A D V A N C E   P R A I S E

"Trauma affects so many of us. It can rob us of a full, meaningful, and joy-filled life. Lilli gets it. She's been there too. She combines her clinical expertise with her own journey to rise above trauma and offers us hope and practical help."

—SUE BERGESON, PRINCIPAL AT RECOVERY, RESILIENCY, ENGAGEMENT AND ACTIVATION PARTNERS, LLC

"Lilli Correll uses her clinical knowledge and her gift of self to get to the heart of the matter—how to be with your past and your pain and then move forward to experience a new level of hope and joy. Her stories and anecdotes are powerful and touching and make the message she has to offer come alive to the reader. This book is a great place to start to get a push in the right direction in the healing process."

—SETH HOUDESHELL, CLINICIAN, CO-AUTHOR OF
*STAYING ON TOP AND KEEPING THE SAND OUT OF YOUR
PANTS: A SURFER'S GUIDE TO THE GOOD LIFE*

"Lilli pours her heart into this personal and honest story about her trauma experience and helps the reader feel supported and hopeful in their own recovery journey."

—JEFF MEYERHOFF, PSYCHIATRIST

"Resolve to Rise provides an insightful and inspirational story of how suffering and trauma can be overcome. Lilli's account of her personal journey fills readers with hope, motivation, and a path forward to face their own challenges and reclaim their lives."

—TRICIA LEA, PHD, MBA, BEHAVIORAL HEALTH EXECUTIVE

"A must-read for anyone wanting to heal after narcissistic abuse. Untangling the mess after narcissistic abuse takes time, work, and self-reflection to heal the wounds caused by the abuse. This book is a comprehensive guide to navigate the healing waters with grace, hope, and love. If you are struggling for validation and looking for a very brave and courageous approach, Correll teaches you through the lessons she learned on her own healing journey."

—TRACY MALONE, AUTHOR, FOUNDER OF NARCISSISTABUSESUPPORT.COM, INTERNATIONAL COACH AND SPEAKER

RESOLVE TO RISE

RESOLVE TO
RISE

Become Greater than Your Circumstances

LILLI CORRELL

LIONCREST
PUBLISHING

RESOLVE TO RISE
Become Greater than Your Circumstances

ISBN   978-1-5445-2474-0 *Hardcover*
       978-1-5445-2473-3 *Paperback*
       978-1-5445-2472-6 *Ebook*
       978-1-5445-2475-7 *Audiobook*

To my family, who has been alongside me on my unfolding journey.

*To Shari, who has been my "balm," healing me with
her kind words and unconditional love.*

To Ashley, who reminds me what resilience and courage look like.

*To Roderick, who strives for excellence and
takes disappointments for learning.*

To Bella, for whom even the sky isn't a limit.

To Tristan and his constant curiosity.

To Lucy and the light she shines for all those around her.

*And to my many friends who have listened to excerpts,
given feedback, encouraged me, and so much more.*

Without them, this book would not have been possible.

CONTENTS

Why is there a bowl on the cover? The bowl was created using a Japanese form of art called Kintsugi.

"Kintsugi is the Japanese art of putting broken pottery pieces back together with gold—built on the idea that in embracing flaws and imperfections, you can create an even stronger, more beautiful piece of art. Every break is unique, and instead of repairing an item like new, the 400-year-old technique actually highlights the 'scars' as a part of the design. Using this as a metaphor for healing ourselves teaches us an important lesson: Sometimes in the process of repairing things that have broken, we actually create something more unique, beautiful, and resilient."[1]

1   Tiffany Ayuda, "How the Japanese art of Kintsugi can help you deal with stressful situations," *NBC*, April 28, 2018, https://www.nbcnews.com/better/health/ how-japanese-art-technique-kintsugi-can-help-you-be-more-ncna866471

INTRODUCTION

I was born in a small town in western Massachusetts. I was the second of two girls and ended up being my mom's favored child, which was no great prize. As she would later tell me, I was "her savior." Over time, I came to believe I was a savior to my whole family. It was my job to calm my mother so no one got hurt. To make matters worse, my father's focus was on my sister, leaving me without anyone who truly saw me.

I wasn't always successful at "my job." Sometimes, no amount of smiling or cutting up with my mom could calm her, and she erupted like a volcano—explosively and with little warning. The violence in our home was so severe that my father was the first man in the state of Massachusetts to win custody of his children. Later, I learned my mother had to have threatened to kill me or my sister to lose primary custody in our state. In our case, she did so in front of a police officer.

As I grew up, I thought I could handle anything that came my way. I was also my own biggest critic. My internal dialogue was often filled with lines like "You need to stop talking" or "You are too sensitive." These were not words of compassion but of criticism. I was constantly measuring myself against others. It was a never-ending battle; I was either better or less than everyone, never just in community with others. My whole life was a competition to feel okay and be enough.

My mom's and dad's words often echoed in my head along with my own internalized negativity, which I rehearsed again and again. I knew I was only increasing my suffering, but whatever I tried, the thoughts just kept coming and tormenting me. Eventually, I began to replay old behaviors in new relationships, taking responsibility for others' happiness. I felt either immense shame or anger when letting others down. It seemed everything was about my adequacy or inadequacy.

Abuse has many negative impacts. It gives the abuser the false impression they are superior, while the abused feels inferior. It often leaves the abused individual with a deep seeded sense of shame—the feeling that they must have done something wrong. If the abused individual does gain the courage to speak out about the abuses they suffered, they are often accused of "playing the victim." In reality, they *were* victimized and are now bravely speaking the truth.

The brain also undergoes significant changes following trauma, especially repeated trauma. A person who has experienced such abuse and trauma often becomes paralyzed or debilitated, carrying a great weight of shame. In turn, they may be more comfortable developing relationships with others who have experienced significant trauma and have difficulty navigating relationships or with others who could retraumatize them.

I wrote this book because I live a life resolved to rise. Life still kicks my ass from time to time. I still make ill-advised decisions that take me off course now and again. But through it all, I keep picking myself up, dusting myself off, and figuring out what will be the healthiest path forward. Because I refuse to let my challenges define me as a person, I continue forward. And now that I have had this resolve for many years, I've accumulated some wisdom along the journey. I'd like to share what I've learned with you.

It is also important to mention that my intention is not to indict my mother or call her out for being a bad parent. I know she suffered her own trauma, and her parents likely did as well. She had her own journey. I can only reflect on what I experienced, how I was impacted, and what I needed to keep going. My intention is to create a path forward for those who want to heal.

This book is an invitation to you to be bold and courageous

in your journey of healing. It is also an instruction guide for how to pick up the pieces of your past and reassemble a life with self-compassion and grace so that you can heal from the deepest hurts that currently hold you captive. Trauma can leave you feeling like you are damaged beyond repair and destined to live a life of dysfunction and pain, so more than anything, **I want to inspire you with hope**!

Throughout the book, I will share about the courage and vulnerability I needed on this journey. I'll also be honest about the sheer terror of it all! The biggest fear you might have is that others will judge you, so my hope is that you read each page and feel increasingly embraced by grace and love.

I hope this book serves as validation for you. Surviving trauma is hard, but it can get better. Rising is not only about dreaming dreams—it's about living out your dreams for a better future. Abuse or trauma may have taken power from you. You may feel you are the problem or that nothing can be done to make life better. I'm here to offer a different story.

I am writing this book as someone who experienced early childhood trauma, but I am also writing as a behavioral health clinician and a certified clinical trauma provider. I have spent my life recovering from the impacts of my trauma (whether direct impacts, like flashbacks, or indirect impacts, like autoimmune disease).

I decided to start writing in a journal when I was eight years old in hopes of improving my perspective and navigating life with greater ease. In my first entry, I wrote down everything I liked about my best friend so I could go back to it whenever I felt angry with her. I used to joke that my journal was my first solution-focused counseling intervention, and the intervention was on myself. I would focus on the positive, and the positive would expand. Throughout this book, I will share excerpts from my journal to show you how I gained new perspective over the years.

I received my master's degree in family psychology and went on to obtain my clinical licensure. I spent nineteen years counseling individuals, couples, and families while I was climbing the ladder in corporate America. I have spent my career with a focus on equipping organizations and individuals for success, always highlighting the importance of showing regard, kitting others for success, being accountable, and holding others accountable. More than anything, I've always wanted to make the world a better place.

My professional and personal hope has been to embrace my journey, learn from the missteps and successes, and advance my goals. Both work and life have given me opportunities to look at myself, learn, and grow. That growth has empowered me with tools to help others advance their hopes and dreams.

As civil rights activist Diane Nash said, "Freedom, by defi-

nition, is people realizing that they are their own leaders."
You cannot remain a victim forever. Eventually, if not all at
once, a restlessness will grow in you to rise up. You then
get to choose what you do with that energy. Sometimes you
might live in reaction to what occurred, becoming angry and
resentful. This response is understandable but will not ultimately produce any benefit. When anger takes up residence
in you, there is no room for healing.

The fact that you are reading this book lets me know you
want to claim the person you were born to be. With this in
mind, I salute you for leaning into your journey and having
the boldness and bravery to look your suffering in the face
and say, "I recognize you and all your impacts, but I am not
a victim anymore. I am wonderfully made and full of possibilities—possibilities that I choose to realize and claim."

As Jackie Chan said, "Life will knock us down, but we can
choose whether or not to stand back up."

I dedicate this book to every person out there who chooses
to stand back up in search of something bigger and fuller
and richer than the perceived limitations set on them by the
challenges they face. I hope this book leaves you with hope
and a path forward.

IMPORTANT NOTE TO THE READER

Although I have extensive clinical experience and training in trauma, the opinions expressed in this book are not intended to be used in lieu of professional counseling. Please be careful about dredging up memories and working through them without proper clinical support. Processing trauma can be retraumatizing. I have limited my sharing of traumatic events to minimize content that might be triggering for you.

Last, I encourage you to take breaks from the work of healing and breathe. Shelve your efforts to rise from time to time and have some fun. I do this by playing tennis, kayaking, spending time with friends, shopping, watching hilarious movies, or even jumping on my pogo stick. Find your own ways to breathe and have fun as you work through this book. This is a journey, and it's important to take it one step at a time.

CHAPTER 1

SUFFERING IS UNIVERSAL

"Wise people don't choose to suffer, but suffering does create wise people."

My first seven years of life were full of much chaos and violence between my parents. My mother suffered from bipolar I disorder with psychosis and had significant mood swings. She would go from joking to terrifying rage within seconds. We often didn't know what set it off.

I learned fairly early on that it was my job to keep things calm. My mom saw me as her savior and looked to me to understand and comfort her. If I failed, all hell broke loose. So I learned that any outburst could be contained if I handled it right; I was responsible.

And because my father thought being my "mother's favorite" protected me in some way from the terrible impacts of abuse, I was often alone in navigating the rough times. He would periodically reflect on his conversation with the psychologist who had been assigned to me during the divorce and say, "I was so stunned when your therapist said, 'Lilli will always have emotional problems. She is terrified of her mother.' I wondered how that could be when you were her favorite. It was your sister that couldn't do anything right."

Even though my father never quite understood the challenges I faced with my mother, I found solace in my relationship with him. I liked to call him Vati (pronounced Fah-tee), which is the German word for "daddy." He was my big teddy bear. Of course, my father wasn't perfect. I suffered because of his inadequacies. But again and again, my father revealed his humanity to me, and in so doing made it okay for me to be human. He instilled in me a sense that I could do whatever I wanted to do, professionally and personally. Despite the fact that he was more protective of my sister, he still delighted in me. As a result, I considered him my best friend. He was the one who moved us away from the violence, so I could easily forgive his shortcomings.

He had struggled with his weight his whole life and was off and on diets and exercise plans. When I was thirty-three years old, he had lost over a hundred pounds and needed surgical help to remove the excess skin. He had a panniculectomy, a surgery to remove the excess skin and tissue from his lower abdomen. The incision was eighty-six inches; that is over seven feet. It put the term "invasive procedure" in a whole new light.

After the surgery, he struggled physically. Some of the bone around his ankle deteriorated so much that he was unable to walk. He was relocated to a powered wheelchair in which he quite literally drove around the town. He was such a gregarious and active person, and being strapped to a wheelchair was unbearable for him. At times, he mentioned feeling deeply depressed and hopeless.

One day, his symptoms became quite severe. He was admitted to the hospital and given tests to figure out the underlying issues causing his immediate symptoms. Before the results were read, the physician ordered a blood thinner. The test results would later reveal my vati was in congestive heart failure, and the last thing he needed was a blood thinner. Before sunrise, he bled out and died. He was sixty-four.

I received the news at work. My best friend, my vati, was gone forever. I hung up the phone and walked around the corner to tell one of my supervisors. As I spoke, my body gave out. "My father is dead." I collapsed on the floor and began to wail. Uncontrollable sobs from the deepest parts of me resounded across the call center. One of the directors came out of his office to see what was happening. He helped me stand up and walked me to his office. I was absolutely devastated, realizing in that moment I would likely spend more of this life without my vati than I had with him. How could that be? What would I do without him? Who would I call when things got rough?

My coworkers and friends were incredibly compassionate. They too had lost loved ones. They too had suffered. I was not alone. In the midst of my pain, I remembered a statistic I had stumbled upon in graduate school: 20 percent of children lose a parent by the age of eighteen. Although the pain felt unbearable for a time, it reminded me of a greater reality: suffering is universal. I wasn't alone in my suffering, and you are not alone in yours.

YOU'RE NOT ALONE

It would take more than one chapter to list out everything that causes stress or suffering. However, it is helpful to consider some of the major events that tend to cause the greatest degrees of suffering. The following is a short list:

- Death of a loved one
- Divorce or separation
- Major illness or injury
- Mental health issues
- Job loss or conflicts with a boss
- Increase in financial obligations

- Taking care of an elderly or sick individual
- Traumatic events
- Retirement

Suffering not only happens; it happens in large numbers every year. Consider the following statistics as you consider how widespread difficult circumstances are:

- DEATH: According to the CDC, more than **2.8 million people died** in 2018. Each death on average results in a **minimum of five people grieving**. Of these people, 40 percent meet the criteria for major depression one month after their loss; 24 percent still meet the criteria after two months.[1]
- DIVORCE/SEPARATION: Nearly **50 percent of all marriages end in divorce** or separation. This stat has become so well known that I don't even need to cite it. We all know it.
- CHRONIC ILLNESS: According to the CDC (2020), six in ten individuals have a chronic condition, and four in ten have multiple chronic conditions.
- MENTAL ILLNESS: In the United States, **one in five have mental illness**, and **one in twenty have serious mental illness**.[2]
- JOB LOSS: In the United States, **9.8 million people are**

---

1   https://www.therecoveryvillage.com/mental-health/grief/related/grief-statistics/

2   https://www.nami.org/mhstats

now unemployed, which is an improvement since April 2020.[3]

- UNINSURED: Kaiser Family Foundation said 28.9 million non-elderly Americans were without insurance in 2019.[4]
- CAREGIVING: According to a Pew research study in 2015, about a quarter (23 percent) of adults ages forty-five to sixty-four care for an aging adult.
- TRAUMA: **60 percent of adults report abuse** or other difficult family circumstances during childhood,[5] and more than **two-thirds of children** report at least one traumatic event by age sixteen.[6]
- DOMESTIC VIOLENCE: One in three women and one in four men have experienced some form of physical violence by an intimate partner.[7]
- WHAT'S MISSING? There are so many more circumstances that cause great stress and suffering, such as discrimination, food insecurity, housing issues, challenges with affording medical treatments, and so much more.

The bottom line is, **people are suffering**. We don't always think about suffering until we experience it or someone

---

3   According to the Economic News Release in April 2021.

4   https://www.kff.org/uninsured/issue-brief/
    key-facts-about-the-uninsured-population/

5   www.nd.gov

6   SAMHSA, 2020.

7   https://ncadv.org/STATISTICS

close to us goes through a difficult time. It is nearly impossible to live for any duration and not experience at least one of the major stressors. The truth is, we all suffer at one point or another, and yet we don't tend to talk about it. We often carry the hurt and pain inside and suffer alone.

Sometimes, in addition to suffering from the event itself, we also feel alone after going through a difficult or traumatic experience. When my first husband died, everyone went on with life as if nothing had happened. To me, it felt like the whole world had stopped and it would have felt wrong to act as if everything was the same. Seeing others continue to move through life so normally and freely made me feel like I was alone in my heaviness. And that contrast in experience made me want to be alone even more, away from others who didn't seem to get how awful life was.

Stressors and difficult experiences can also be debilitating and result in depression. At some point, we gain resilience and keep moving ahead, but that can take time. Often, finding meaning in the suffering is what helps us move on with life. So many have risen after despair and have created the miraculous things we see around us every day. You too have likely learned to find joy after suffering loss or disappointment.

SHARING AND HEALING

I like to say, "There is an upside to the downside." This is not to diminish the suffering itself. It's important to grieve and process through the suffering. That said, difficult experiences often can, and do, lead to something we might not expect. When things happen that we cannot explain, we see later on in life how it may be for our own good or someone else's. I have had this experience more than a time or two.

Back in late 1993, after a long day at work, I drove to the day care center to pick up my son. He was eighteen months old and not in the happiest of moods that day. From the back seat, he let me know, plainly, he wanted a snack. I had just left the center and was rolling forward at about ten miles per hour when I leaned forward to grab his crackers off the floor.

As I came up with the crackers in my hand, I made contact with a young lady who had been walking in the street. Her body rolled up on my car and hit my windshield, making a dent in the glass where her head hit. I came to an abrupt stop, jumped out of my car, and ran around, gasping for air as I uttered, "I'm sorry, I'm sorry. Are you okay?"

She was quite stunned as she got up, and I was devastated. What had I done? What kind of an idiot was I to take my eyes completely off the road while driving? I was so frightened I peed in my pants. I was likely about six months pregnant with my second child, and all I could think about was the pain I had caused this young woman and her poor parents who would be so concerned and upset. The girl was checked out at the ER and was fine. No broken bones and no internal damage. Thank goodness!

Years later, a client told me she had hit her niece with her car and taken her life. It had been years since the event, but she couldn't forgive herself. She lamented the tragedy. Her niece was her favorite. They spent so much cherished time together, and she was the one responsible for her death. She couldn't let it go.

I gave her all kinds of what I believed to be sage advice about grief and loss. I validated her pain. I listened. I shared Elisabeth Kübler-Ross's stages of grief. I explained that we all go through five stages—denial, anger, bargaining, depression, and acceptance—and that they may not happen in that exact order but that people often repeat stages as they work through the loss. Finally, I shared my story about hitting an eighteen-year-old with my car.

A couple of weeks passed, and we had our last session together. She said, "When I got off the phone with you, I called my mom. 'Mom, you aren't going to believe this,' I said. 'My counselor hit a girl.'" All the wise advice I thought I had given her didn't mean anything; instead, it was my story that meant something. It gave her permission to let herself off the hook. She explained she was much improved since our discussion. As I hung up the phone, I realized that sometimes the pain and suffering we experience becomes the inspiration for hope and healing for someone else.

I encourage you to be vulnerable and share your stories openly with others who may be suffering. Being transparent and sharing your journey enables others to do the same. Doing so removes the walls between us and reconnects us to each other and ourselves. Our words to each other can change the trajectory of our suffering. Healing can come in the form of a friend guiding us in some special way. It can come through a special encounter or even a dream. Regardless, we must remember we are never alone in suffering.

The best way to avoid being alone in your suffering is to find safe people with whom you can share. No matter what you have gone through, others have likely experienced similar feelings and challenges. My father died just four months after my mother. Although I was much closer with my father, I was grieving both of their deaths. I decided to join a hospice support group for a while, and it made all the difference.

The group helped me work through my grief one step at a time. While I was in the group, I found out my father died as the result of a physician's mistake. It was as if I was starting the grieving process all over again, but now I had others who could come around me. They shared similar feelings and were supportive of me in my journey to healing. At least once a week, I knew I was not alone—that others could relate and truly see me and what I was experiencing.

MY JOURNEY UNFOLDING THROUGH MY JOURNALS

I found out about a concept called terminal uniqueness through a twelve-step program. It is a belief that your experiences are unlike anything anyone else has experienced. This type of thinking can reinforce the belief that you can't share openly and leave you feeling isolated and alone. I began to realize I was not alone in my thoughts and feelings by sitting in twelve-step meetings, listening, and sharing openly.

In 1986, I hit an all-time low in my life. I was drinking excessively and doing everything I could to avoid feeling. It occurred to me I needed help and didn't want to live my life as I had been living it. I often wrote about being lonely and was clearly still trying to find love in relationships. I was developing insight through twelve-step support and thought I needed counseling.

October 1986:

The topic at the 10 o'clock meeting was fear. I shared. My fear is of finding out who I am. I'd really rather not look at myself. It scares me.

CHAPTER 2

TRAUMA AND ITS IMPACTS

Trauma comes in all shapes and sizes. It has less to do with the incident and more to do with the person's reaction to the incident—both how it is internalized and how it manifests in changes in the mind and body.

For the first five years of my life, my family lived on a farm where we had fifty-two goats producing milk. When I was four years old, my mom, my sister, and I were all in the house together when the phone rang. My sister took the call. It was a neighbor interested in buying some of our goat's milk. My mom was on a tirade. I don't know what set her off that day. (I often didn't.) What I do know is the noise produced by her raging antics resulted in our neighbor calling my father and letting him know of the situation at home. After he hung up the phone with our neighbor, my father called the police and headed to our house. My sister made her way outside, and my mother took me to an upstairs bedroom.

My father and the first police officer arrived around the same time. My mom stood near the window, yelling profanities. "I am going to kill you and my children," she shouted at my father. Then she addressed the police officer. "And I'll cut you up into pieces and bury you in your potato patch." (As I understand, the police officer did have a potato patch.) At that moment, she reached down and swept me off the floor and flung me across the room and against the wall. Another police officer joined the first and they continued to plead with my mom to come out of the house.

I was terrified and thought I was in trouble. From my limited perspective, I believed I was the reason the police officer was there. I did not mean to cause my mom such unwieldy rage and instead tried to bring nothing but joy. It was repeated experiences like this that led me to fear my mother deeply, and yet I felt responsible to calm her. In my mind, I was saving our lives. It wasn't long after that particular incident that my parents divorced. Still, the turbulent dynamics with my mother persisted.

After a few concerning visits with my mom, my father moved me and my sister to Texas. It was several years before I started going to stay with her each summer for a few weeks.

The summer of my seventeenth birthday, I went to stay with her for an entire summer, which I had not done before. Her mood during my visit was fairly stable, but I was on high alert, ready for any slight shift, ready to calm the situation and make sure her rage was kept at a minimum. I could tell she still tended to react unexpectedly and without provocation.

One day, my mom, my sister, and I went to the grocery store. We had filled our cart and lined up to check out. The cashier started taking one item at a time and moving it to the end of the counter for bagging. As the items started accumulating, I could feel my mom's tension rising. I wasn't sure what set her off, but I quickly stepped up and said, "Mom, can I help bag the groceries?" She turned to me with fury in her eyes and snapped, "No. Get out of my way. I don't need your help. You are just causing more issues." It felt like I had caused only further disruption, and I shrank away from her and out of the way.

Just then, the woman behind us in line leaned forward and whispered in my ear, "This is abuse. Are you okay?"

I was surprised at her words. To me, this was nothing, and I responded with this subtle sense of pride. "I'm fine. Everything is okay." After all, it was my job to make sure everything was okay.

"Well, you don't have to go home with her," she continued as she reached into her pocket for a dime. "Here is a dime for the pay phone," she said. "If you want to call for help, there are people who can help you." I took the dime, thrust it into my pocket, turned, and followed my mom out of the grocery store, glancing at the pay phone as I made my way out. As I left, I wondered what the woman was thinking. What made her see that situation as abuse? After all, I thought, I had it in hand. I knew how to deal with my mom.

I was covered from head to toe with embarrassment and a feeling that I had somehow let the cat out of the bag, revealing to others that there was something wrong with my family. I had mixed emotions between feeling validated and shamed by a complete stranger.

YOUR EXPERIENCE IS VALID

Many of my experiences taught me to disregard my own feelings of fear and take care of the very person who was causing harm. That dynamic created confusion and negative patterns I would replay in my relationships, even into adulthood. Of course, this has also given me the opportunity to learn and grow. The first step was to recognize my experience and feelings as valid. I would later realize the woman saw something I could not see because my sense of "normal" had become so skewed. This is the nature of trauma and abuse: it causes confusion, and it takes time to unravel the complex effects it has on us.

According to the American Psychological Association (APA) as of 2008, 66 percent of children and youths have been victimized by abuse and between 25 and 43 percent have experienced the trauma of sexual abuse. In 2020, the Substance Abuse and Mental Health Services Administration (SAMHSA) reported that more than two-thirds of children witnessed a traumatic event by age sixteen.

The statistics are not as important as what the rates of occurrence tell us—that **many are victimized, but few talk about it**. As with suffering in general, we tend to carry pain from trauma in secrecy, which ultimately isolates us and keeps us from healing. This is especially true of abuse, as abused individuals often carry significant shame that reinforces the need to be quiet.

The National Center for PTSD shows similar statistics. In 2019, the center reported six in ten men and five in ten women (of those surveyed) had suffered at least one trauma in their lives. Those who suffer abuse do not always develop symptoms of post-traumatic stress disorder (PTSD); however, you are more likely to suffer from PTSD if you were injured in some way.

Although my trauma was directly connected to abuse, we can experience trauma in many ways. The National Child Traumatic Stress Network lists the following distinct types of trauma:

- Bullying: Repeated cruelty inflicted on a vulnerable person
- Community violence: Violence seen in a public area by a person not related or known to the victim
- Complex trauma: A child's repeated exposure to traumatic events with both short- and long-term impacts
- Disasters: Natural disasters like hurricanes, tsunamis, etc.
- Early childhood trauma: Trauma that occurs before age six
- Traumatic grief: A child's extreme responses to the loss of a loved one
- Intimate partner violence
- Medical trauma
- Physical abuse
- Sexual abuse
- Refugee trauma
- Terrorism and violence

I am generally exploring the impacts to individuals who suffer from complex trauma, early childhood trauma, physical abuse, and sexual abuse. However, many of the principles can be applied regardless of your specific experience. If you experienced something traumatizing, then for you, it was trauma. If an event or events made you feel "intensely threatened," then you have experienced trauma. This could include a serious motor vehicle accident.

It is important that you not judge whether your experience

should be considered "trauma." Instead, honor the fact that the event left a significant impact on you and seek healing.

Not only do traumatic events make you feel intense emotions, but they can also cause physical reactions, such as an unsettled stomach or headache. If I am intensely triggered, it is not uncommon for me to feel like my body is completely clearing out my bowels as I visit the bathroom again and again. At first, I did not make the connection between my trauma, triggers of my trauma, and gastrointestinal symptoms, but as I exercised more awareness, I noticed the two happen together without fail. You may experience other effects—both mental and physical. We'll explore these for the remainder of the chapter.

MENTAL AND PHYSICAL EFFECTS

Trauma actually changes your brain. Time and time again, research shows three parts of the brain that change when people suffer a trauma:

- The hippocampus shrinks. This is the center for emotion and memory.
- The amygdala function increases. This is the center for creativity and rumination.
- The prefrontal/anterior cingulate function decreases. This is the center for more complex functions such as planning and self-development.

Because traumatic memories are stored in the amygdala, the amygdala will be triggered whenever there is a perceived threat. Many who experience trauma might freeze when there is a perceived threat. The threat may not be real, but it feels real. When this happens, we use what Dan Siegel, a clinical professor of psychiatry at UCLA School of Medicine, refers to as our "downstairs brain" and we react defensively rather than with curiosity. Our reactions in this state will be characterized by anger or fear.

In *The Body Keeps Score*, Bessel van der Kolk outlines how trauma changes the brain and impacts how your current reality is experienced. Life passes you by as you're stuck in the past. Your brain does not allow you to be fully engaged in the present. For some people, trauma becomes a part of their identity. You may find that what turns others off or excites them doesn't impact you. You might also find that parts of yourself are exiled while other aspects are enhanced.

For instance, you may suppress your weaknesses and emphasize your anger. When you address the parts of you that have been put aside, you tend to grow in wisdom and insight. Exploring feelings or situations you have avoided will increase your learning about yourself and lessen your need to avoid certain circumstances, ultimately giving you more freedom.

Symptoms of trauma can be immediate and long term. Some

are caused by the immediate reaction you have to the trauma, and others are caused by high levels of stress and reactivity in your body. According to van der Kolk, if trauma started before age fourteen, symptoms may include:

- Affect regulation (77 percent likelihood): Difficulty regulating emotional reactions, extreme reactions, or swings in emotions
- Anger (77 percent likelihood): Difficulty calming down when angry
- Self-destructive behavior (62 percent likelihood): Could include substance use or abuse or self-harming behaviors
- Suicidal thoughts (66 percent likelihood)
- Sexual involvement (81 percent likelihood): Risk-taking behavior involving sexual activity
- Risk taking (54 percent likelihood): Want to be seen as a daredevil by taking big risks
- Amnesia (78 percent likelihood): Cannot remember parts of your life
- Dissociation (80 percent likelihood)
- Permanent damage (72 percent likelihood): May look at yourself as damaged goods or broken
- Guilt (69 percent likelihood): Tendency to feel guilty when anything goes wrong, whether it's your fault or not
- Shame (60 percent likelihood)
- Isolation (80 percent likelihood): Feeling like no one understands and you are alone

- Digestive problems (69 percent likelihood)
- Hopelessness (75 percent likelihood)
- Loss of trust (71 percent likelihood)
- Minimizing (28 percent likelihood): Believe you are making what happened too big of an issue

There are more symptoms identified by van der Kolk. If you are interested in them, you can research DESNOS symptoms.

When clinicians are diagnosing PTSD, they use a reference called the *Diagnostic and Statistical Manual of Mental Disorders*, 5th Edition: DSM-5. The following list includes symptoms individuals experience after trauma. Most people will have at least some of these:

- Nightmares, usually quite vivid
- Unwanted and upsetting memories
- Physical reactions to reminders of the traumatic incident
- Flashbacks of the incident—sometimes in the body (feelings without visualizations), sometimes visual memories, and sometimes a combination
- Avoidance of situations or thoughts and feelings that may remind you of the traumatic event
- Inability to remember aspects of the traumatic event
- Difficulty feeling positive emotions and a tendency toward negative emotions

- Intrusive thoughts or images
- Changes in memory and concentration
- Difficulty sleeping
- Hypervigilance or jumpiness
- Difficulty concentrating
- Overly negative thoughts and beliefs about oneself and the world
- Unemotional state, feeling cut off from emotions, or numbness
- Hypersensitivity to particular situations, smells, sounds, or sensations, especially those that remind you of the incident
- Difficulty maintaining closeness with others over time (i.e., feel close initially and feel less connected as time goes on)
- Difficulty enjoying things you used to enjoy
- Obsessive-compulsive tendencies, feeling a need to ensure certain things happen, or obsessively thinking about something (e.g., belief you have to get into the car within four minutes or you will be in an accident)
- Irritability
- Feeling alone
- Risk taking or self-destructive behavior
- Chronic feelings of emptiness

In addition to emotional impacts of trauma, individuals have an increased risk of health conditions resulting from prolonged stress. Dr. Matthew Tull outlines the impacts in an

article called "How PTSD Relates to Physical Health Issues."
He outlines the following related conditions:

- Gastrointestinal problems
- Arthritis
- Diabetes
- Reproductive problems
- Breathing problems
- Heart disease
- Pain
- Autoimmune disease (which was noted in a 2020 article in *Healthline* called "The Link between Autoimmune Diseases and PTSD")

There are so many possible symptoms from trauma that it would be nearly impossible to convey them all. Furthermore, we, like snowflakes, are unique and the impact of trauma will look different for each of us. You cannot say, "Oh, you experienced trauma, then you must…" It's better to avoid making comparisons.

There are, however, symptoms that are more common, such as dissociation. If you experience dissociation, you may lose periods of time or not remember doing certain things. You might seem absent to others, like you are somewhere else and not present. You might not be able to remember the trauma or have gaps in your memory. Other symptoms are less common, such as tics (involuntary muscle contractions typically produced by prolonged stress, similar to a startle response).

WHERE YOU GO FROM HERE

There are many trauma screenings out there. The most commonly known screening for adults is called ACEs, or Adverse Childhood Experiences. The children's version is called PEARLS, or Pediatric ACEs and Related Life-Events Screener. The questionnaires essentially add up early childhood abuse into a score that indicates the likelihood of long-term impacts, both to mental health and physical health. Evidence indicates the higher the score, the greater the effects.

If you are interested in understanding if you dissociate, you can also look into the Dissociative Experiences Scale (DES). They have one for adults, adolescents, and children. The screenings don't measure a person's resilience or ability to heal from trauma. Resilience and health are also improved greatly when a child has at least one stable and safe relationship early in life.

As you move toward healing, understand that the responses you've had to trauma are normal. Viktor Frankl was an Austrian Holocaust survivor who suffered great horrors in a concentration camp. He said, "An abnormal reaction to an abnormal situation is normal behavior." To react as you normally would to terrifying acts is abnormal. If you experience trauma and then have ill effects, you are actually normal—not the other way around.

Next, recognize the choices you have now. One thing Viktor Frankl and many survivors of trauma have is resilience. He said, "Everything can be taken from a man but one thing: the last of the human freedoms—to choose one's attitude in any given set of circumstances, to choose one's own way." Frankl's approach to his own horror was to create an inner sanctuary where he could keep his hopes and dreams safe. What we learn from Frankl and from our own suffering is that we can move through the pain and suffering into hope and strength.

MY JOURNEY UNFOLDING THROUGH MY JOURNALS

In May 2005, I was diagnosed with multiple sclerosis and was beginning to realize I wasn't actually a hypochondriac, as I had thought. I was the opposite, always belittling my actual symptoms. I never thought there was ever anything wrong with me and was embarrassed when I had to explain my symptoms to the doctor, thinking they would tell me I was wrong. After all, I had learned not to trust myself. It was in sharing openly with friends, doctors, and my therapist that I realized I could trust myself. During this time, I wrote the following in my journal:

May 2005:

On Tuesday, a week after my first neurology appointment, I was in my therapist's office giving her my "data dump" from my job promotion on Friday and the Monday diagnosis and following medical treatment. Then I extended my legs and laid back into the sofa. A few tears started coming and I said, "I'm tired. God has created a situation that I can't possibly handle on my own and the only leap is surrendering to His will, and I don't know how." I have spent years staying on top of everything the best I could, but I wasn't going to be able to this time.

CHAPTER 3

GOOD MORNING, GRACE!

As we go through our own healing journeys, processing through the suffering and trauma we've experienced, we can often feel stuck because of the heavy weight of shame. It is important to have approaches to address and minimize feelings of shame so you can move forward more easily.

Growing up as "a savior," I believed that the world was an unsafe place unless I helped calm and address others' needs. My needs were not a priority. Somewhere along the way, I stopped connecting to and listening to what I needed. Instead, whenever I felt tension, I tried to quickly assess what someone else needed. Usually, that person was my mom. My nervous system reacted as if every situation that arose was life and death, and the key to making it out alive was my ability to read the needs of the other person and successfully address their needs. On the other hand, I did not trust anyone to meet my needs. Heck, I did not even know what my needs were.

When I searched through my journals dating back to when I was thirteen years old, the word "shame" came up again and again and again. Shame at being associated with my mother and her behavior. Shame for things I had done. Shame for having wounds from trauma. And sometimes shame because of my humanity, though I later realized my inadequacy was not uniquely bad or detestable. Had I realized that being human means being imperfect and that I was not alone, I might have extended myself more generosity and compassion.

After working as a therapist for nearly twenty years and supporting many other people in their healing journey outside of counseling, I realized that much of what we feel and think is the same. There is little that is "new under the sun." We all tend to highlight our triumphs and keep what burdens us in the dark.

The reality is that our suffering and difficult experiences do not disqualify us from life and relationships; they can actually make us better equipped. Some cultures understand this reality better than others. For example, shamans see suffering and overcoming adversity as an initiation, making them "wounded healers." They believe that not going through such difficulty limits the practitioner.

For many of us, we'd rather avoid difficult experiences and feelings. After all, who can we trust? When we experience suffering and trauma, we may not feel safe enough to be vulnerable. But if we want to heal and move past shame, we will have to grow in our ability to trust.

LEARNING TO TRUST

I lived on an island of sorts that protected me from others and kept me safe from vulnerability. So when I made a dear friend who truly listened and cared about what I had to say, I was afraid to trust. But I realized if I stayed on my island and did not let her in, I could stay self-sufficient and apparently safe but ultimately alone. I didn't even admit to myself that I didn't like how alone I felt. I had spent a lifetime talking myself through pain and analyzing my way into what seemed like healthy behavior.

One day, we were riding to lunch, and she was asking me what was wrong. I realized I could act tough and imply nothing was wrong, or I could share what was going on inside and take a risk. If I did as I had always done, I felt I wouldn't be hurt. I would remain impenetrable, but oh yeah, I would also be alone. My first response was, "Why are you always so nice to me?" She seemed somewhat surprised by my question but responded empathetically, "Because I care." I sat in silence as we drove, realizing I had never accepted someone caring for me. I didn't trust it. I had held everyone at a distance to some degree.

I had a choice. I was terrified of being vulnerable, and yet I didn't want to continue as I had. So when we arrived at lunch, I told her what was going on. I risked everything and shared that I had spent a lifetime on an emotional island, not trusting anyone. I also told her I recognized how she truly cared for me as a person.

In that moment, I made a choice to move off my island. I knew that if I didn't, I might be safe emotionally, but I would also be alone and never truly close to anyone. If I risked coming off the island, I might get hurt, but I also might experience real healing. So I took the leap and shared openly; I was vulnerable.

It was shame that kept me on the island and the sincere grace my friend extended me that encouraged me to leave it. Her grace was life-changing for me.

UNDERSTANDING SHAME, THE BARRIER TO TRUST

If the person who is supposed to protect you is harming you, you tend to believe you are the problem. Our shame increases when others around us ask us to change rather than address the abusive or dysfunctional behavior in someone else. This pattern occurs because it's easier for everyone to keep things as they are.

In family systems therapy, we refer to this pattern as homeostasis. It works like the heater or air-conditioner in a home. If the heater is set at 67 degrees, and the temperature falls below 67, the heater will kick on to bring the temperature back up. In families, family members want things to stay constant and will do almost anything to ensure that is the case. When a child says they were abused by a family member, the entire family must respond. Things are out of balance, and the family members work to resume relational harmony.

Therefore, even though statistics show us 98 percent of children are telling the truth when they make an outcry of abuse,[8] siblings and family members often do not believe them. Similarly, one in three adults would not believe a child if they disclosed sexual abuse.[9] Some might not respond because of the bystander effect. They might witness an event and do nothing to intervene, expecting someone else to act.

It's actually more common for children to lie in saying

8   NSW Child Protection Council, cited in Dympna House 1998, https://www.facs.nsw.gov.au/providers/children-families/child-protection-services.

9   Australian Childhood Foundation, 2010, https://www.childhood.org.au/~/media/Files/Research/Research%2520Doing%2520Nothing%2520Hurts%2520Children.

abuse did not happen than it is for a child to make a false accusation. Consider the fact that 60 percent of victims of sexual abuse never tell anyone, and 10 percent of children are sexually abused by age eighteen.[10] This stat is telling but unfortunately not surprising. To say the world oftentimes doesn't respond with compassion and grace is an understatement. Many people stand idly by, doing nothing, refusing to believe, or actively dismissing. As a result, a victim of abuse will often suck it down, disconnect, and try to act as if everything is normal. They will even internalize the response to the abuse, transforming it into shame.

Shame alienates you (and me) from others and says you are different and inadequate. It tells you that you are unworthy of any and all goodness and are in some way less than others. And it spurs on your urge to keep your shortcomings and challenges to yourself, further separating you from community.

As I have shared my stories and found that so many others feel and think the same way as I do, I have been freed up to heal. That's why it was important to me to set the stage: suffering and trauma are all too common, and the impacts are various and deep. When you realize many people suffer and are walking around as you have, concealing the undesirable parts of their stories, you realize how shame keeps us from each other. Here are a few important points to understand about shame:

10 Child Sexual Abuse Statistics, in Darkness to Light publication in 2015.

- Shame has an impact. Shame can be a debilitating emotion in which you see yourself as incompetent, which results in feeling stuck and unable to move forward. It has a paralyzing effect.
- Shame is not the same as embarrassment. Embarrassment happens to everyone and is momentary. You might trip up the stairs and feel embarrassed in the moment. Shame is a broader belief about oneself as flawed. Instead of thinking, *That was embarrassing*, you think, *I am embarrassing*.
- No one deserves to be abused. It is important to realize the abuse wasn't your fault, and you didn't invent or exaggerate it. Abuse is abuse, trauma is trauma, and intense feelings and shame are normal responses to mistreatment or abuse. No one can tell you that you are overstating things because it is *your* feelings and *your* experience, and they are valid.

My shame became such a constant companion in my life that I hardly even noticed it anymore. I was surprised when others would say, "You are so hard on yourself." I wasn't sure how they knew. One friend said to me, "You really need to stop apologizing." So I wrote myself a note that said, "Be appreciative rather than apologetic," and I glanced at it several times each day. It made it clear to me how often I apologized. I was apologizing for this and that all day long.

As you begin to respond to shame, I cannot express enough

the power of having people believe and support you. I recently came across someone who had suffered awful abuse. When asked if she struggled with shame, she said, "No. I haven't because of the people I have in my life that believe and support me." Being told that your feelings and experiences are normal given what you suffered and having people believe you knocks down barriers created by shame and keeps them from erecting in the first place.

It's important to understand that there's no such thing as a single step to healing. You will not experience triggers once, solve them, and then have nothing trigger you again. Healing is a process, and it is critical that we start in a space of self-love and compassion. What we suffered had real impacts. We experience these impacts not because we're flawed but because we're human. If you beat yourself about the head because of what you feel, it turns into humiliation, and you'll come full circle back to shame. For these reasons, it's critical that you learn to have grace with yourself.

START WITH GRACE

You are still precious, just as you were as a child, but now you are in the driver's seat deciding which way you will go. Start with grace, understanding the journey will be replete with setbacks and triumphs. Don't let the setbacks prompt you to give up. Acknowledge them, acknowledge the feelings they produce, show yourself compassion (of course you are disappointed and want to give up), and remind yourself that you are worth every effort.

GRACE: Give Respect, Acceptance, and Compassion Every day.

Give: Give to yourself as you do to others; like oxygen on an airplane, start with yourself first and then extend it to others.

Give **Respect**: Show respect to yourself for what you have navigated. You are not damaged and disqualified; you have made it this far. That speaks volumes to your perseverance, regardless of how discouraged you may have felt in the process. Some days, just getting out of bed is a success.

Give **Acceptance**: You are where you are. You cannot change where you are, what you face, or what still plagues you. Fighting it or telling yourself you should be some way that you are not just makes you struggle more. In fact, recognizing there is a problem is the first step to solving it. Take a moment to celebrate your bravery in looking at the hard stuff before dealing with it. And if you notice you have made a big mistake or handled things poorly, **celebrate your awareness**.

Give **Compassion**: Speak to yourself as kindly as you speak to others, with less critique. If compassion is to feel a deep sense of empathy for someone else's suffering, what would it look like for you to give yourself compassion? This would involve looking at what happened to you and mourning over the way you've struggled. It might involve being kind to yourself when you notice you're triggered and upset. Instead of responding with self-criticism, figure out what you need to do to take care of yourself.

Every day: Recommit every day to be more aware and actively show yourself kindness.

Here are some ways to give GRACE to yourself:

- Consider the abuse you suffered and the age you were, and think of a child you know experiencing the same thing at the same age. Do you blame them? Do you think less of them for the way it would impact them?
- Watch your self-talk. Are you being critical? Are you highlighting every misstep and blunder? Do you tell yourself you are doing a good job? Do you highlight the successes? Avoid saying things to yourself that you think would be cruel or unsupportive to say to someone else. We are often our own worst critics. I was on a call with a friend the other day and she said, "I'm an idiot." She is so generous and giving and yet that's what she tells herself. She would *never* say that to someone else. She likely doesn't even entertain thoughts about others that are that negative, and yet when it comes to herself, she gives the harshest criticism.
- Spend time with people and friends who are affirming and supportive to you.

- Meditate. I started with guided meditation and still use it often because my brain is so active. It helps me to have something to focus on during the exercise.
- Remember: positive out, positive in. When you make it a point to brighten others' days, yours will be brighter too. When you are generous, generosity comes back to you. And by generous, I mean taking a moment to tell others what you appreciate about them or simply smiling at them. Or asking, "How are you doing?" and listening to the answer.
- Set limits. Not only is it okay to say no, but it is important that you do. Sometimes the most compassionate thing we can do is clearly establish and honor our and others' boundaries. Henry Cloud, clinical psychologist and co-author of *Boundaries*, wrote, "If we feel responsible for other people's feelings, we can no longer make decisions based on what is right; we will make decisions based on how others feel about our choices."
- Make a list of what you like about yourself and accomplishments you have achieved.
- Do things for yourself. Find activities that help you feel supported.
- Make time to have fun. You may have experienced trauma, but you are not the trauma. Be careful not to orient your life around bad things that have happened to you. More specifically, take breaks from addressing your trauma and do things that give your life color, such as sports, dance, or having fun with friends.

In addition to employing various approaches to developing greater self-love, I have found it particularly helpful to work with a counselor and have close friends who are on their own healing journeys. They can support me in mine and I can support them in theirs. Both friends and counselors have helped me understand my negative self-talk and supported me in extending myself more grace on a regular basis.

As far as counseling, there are many different approaches and evidence-based practices out there for the treatment of trauma, each developed based on how trauma impacts a person. Research shows that trauma impacts the mind and body, so therapy to address it should involve both. I have included some insights into various approaches to treating trauma in the Appendixes.

Oftentimes, talk therapy is used to address the results of abuse with minimal effect. After years of talk therapy and noticing the same struggles arise, you can feel even more discouraged and broken beyond repair. The truth is, your body experienced the trauma, which is what changed your brain. The reaction happens in a part of your brain that is referred to as the reptilian brain. You didn't consciously make a decision to fight, flee, or freeze; you responded instinctually because of a perceived threat. The problem is that you still experience what happened in the past as if it is the present. Engaging the body in therapy helps you stay in the present. The therapeutic process should ultimately minimize the sense of threat.

MY JOURNEY UNFOLDING THROUGH MY JOURNALS

In 2017, I realized that I think and talk my way through stressful events in my life. It is part of my island living. I often feel like I don't need anyone because I am an island unto myself. As a result, I think and talk my way out of feeling and connecting.

January 2017:

By my very nature, I tend to analyze things; break them down, reconstruct them, break them down again, and put them back together. I want to understand how things fundamentally work; how one thing impacts another; what other options there are. So it's not too difficult to extrapolate from that idea that I might at times take up residence in my head and therefore spend little time naturally just giving the thinking a rest.

When I'm running, I'm looking around at things and people. For instance, I'll see a man who appears to be running with a slight limp. I'll watch his gait and break down his movement. I'll make a conclusion—I think his right leg is slightly shorter than his left. I wonder how that might impact his muscles, set him up for injury. Would a shoe insert correct the problem?... And the mental chatter goes on and on.

My spouse says, "Where are you? You don't seem present." And then I think, "Am I present? I'm analyzing what I'm seeing in this moment."...And off I go on another mental chatter exercise.

*This would all be fine, and people might think I'm quite intelligent and inquisitive, but **it strips me of my ability to connect**.*

It was because of this realization that I started to meditate more regularly—and not just any meditation but guided meditation. I found that listening to ocean waves or sitting silently was tough for me. Instead of having a profound meditative experience, I was making my grocery list and plans for the week. I had never embraced meditation as a regular practice, saying I couldn't do it because my mind is too busy. That's similar to the mentality that you can't call a cleaning lady to your house because you have to clean it first.

Finally, I discovered a meditation by Sharon Salzberg. As I sat with my eyes closed, listening for her prompts and trying to center myself on my breath, she said, "Isn't it amazing [that] no matter what, we can begin again? We might end up far, far away for a long time, and still there is that moment. We say that the healing is in the return, not in never having wandered to begin with. As we let go gently and with great kindness toward ourselves, we begin again."

This was a profound concept for me, that becoming distracted was not negative but positive. Because it took awareness to realize my mind had wandered. And I began to contemplate what that kind of perspective would do to each day if I just considered that every time. I discovered that if I made a mistake, I could see it as a chance to show up differently, a guidepost of sorts—like a DO NOT ENTER sign.

This awareness has been extremely helpful to me. Sometimes things start falling apart for me, I notice my self-critic is back in the driver's seat, and I'm again disconnected from those around me and deeply engaged in thought. When I notice it now, I realize it is not the time to further criticize myself but to simply take note that I have neglected the positive habits and slipped back into old behaviors. Then I have a chance to choose how I will proceed. For me, this might mean journaling, meditating, spending time with friends, or spending time alone. There are so many possibilities now that I've accumulated a list of strategies. I can employ them and see a positive difference, and I continue to try new things.

In listening to Sharon's meditation, I was extending myself grace. I knew silent meditation was too difficult for me and decided it was okay; I could listen to guided meditation. And then her guidance gave me insights for my life. The change from kicking myself when I'm down to extending a hand so I can stand back up makes all the difference. When shame rears its ugly head, know that it does that for all of us who are healing from trauma, and give yourself GRACE.

CHAPTER 4

"GOING ON A BEAR HUNT"

There have been times I've looked at my trauma out of the corner of my eye and said, "I cannot face it. I just want to move on." Nevertheless, when I face what needs to be faced, I am better for it. In the children's book *We're Going on a Bear Hunt*, author Michael Rosen explains, "We can't go over it. We can't go under it. We've got to go through it." Rosen describes one unpleasant circumstance after the next, and again and again he says, "We've got to go through it."

My life has taught me the truth of this sentiment. I must go through it. And oh, how I want to skip past it so as not to be vulnerable or face more pain. When I was twenty-five years old, I realized just how difficult—and important—it is to walk through the pain and not try to go around it.

At the time, my husband and I had just moved to Abilene, Texas, so I could start my graduate studies. He had started working at the local hospital, and I had started school. We lived in offsite student housing and began to develop friendships.

It was late one night when he arrived home from work. Our children were snuggled in their beds asleep. Earlier that day, we had taken the children to the local mall. He played a turbo race car game with the children, sliding back and forth and giggling all the while, and we got lunch as a family. As the outing progressed, he seemed almost sluggish, and I was a little frustrated he wasn't more energized during our outing.

He changed out of his work clothes, took a shower, and got into bed. "Lilli," he asked, "will you scratch my shoulders?" Then he rolled over and rubbed my feet first. He kept falling asleep, so I told him not to worry and I would do it myself. In all honesty, we fell asleep before I got around to scratching his back. During the night, I would remember later, I heard him snoring in and out as he slept.

I awoke the next morning as the sun shone through the window, and the children came to our bedside as they always did. As I arose, I realized something wasn't right. My husband seemed very still. I don't remember anything about the children at this point, as my focus was entirely devoted to my husband. "Todd," I said, "wake up!" There was no response and total stillness. I reached out and grabbed the phone as I went around the bed. I touched him, and he was unresponsive. As I called 911, I continued to try to wake him. "Todd...Todd..."

"911, please state your emergency" came through the phone.

I quickly explained something was very wrong. I could not wake my husband. Then with every bit of strength I could muster, I pushed his over 200-pound body over on our waveless waterbed. It took everything in me, but I finally got him turned over. "There are bubbles!" I exclaimed. "I think he's alive. I'll give him CPR." Only there was no response to CPR.

A few minutes passed, and the EMTs arrived and pronounced him dead. "How could that be?" I said. "I'm only twenty-five! I'm only twenty-five! I don't understand. I'm only twenty-five." I went to my neighbor's house with my children. I was knocking on her door, then her windows, then her door, earnestly trying to get her to answer. It seemed like hours before she responded, although it was likely no more than five minutes. She opened the door, and the children and I went into their house and sat on the couch. I told them what happened and then called one of the few friends I had made since our arrival. She rushed over to my neighbor's house.

"Lilli," she said, "we need to go back in the house."

As I shivered with adrenaline, I mustered, "Are you sure? I'm scared."

"Yes," she said.

I didn't know what the right thing to do was in these circumstances, so I followed her lead.

Once we got into the house, she said, "Lilli, we need to go into the bedroom."

Again, I said, "But I'm afraid." And yet I followed her in complete trust.

She went with me back into the master bedroom, where just hours before I found my husband and companion dead. Then she urged me to strip the bed. As I did, I expressed my immense grief and pounded my fists on the bed. I cried and screamed, "How could you leave me? I'm only twenty-five. I can't raise our children alone. No!" I could feel great surges of energy run through my body as I pounded my fists, and tears streamed down my face. "No!" And then I was exhausted and somehow settled for the time being.

Months later, I found out my husband had developed an enlarged heart, something we had no idea was present. That fateful evening, his heart had reached its capacity. He was thirty-four when he passed away.

At around the same time my husband died, one of my friends from high school lost his wife just after she birthed their second child. My friend, by contrast, went home and went to great lengths to avoid driving by the hospital. I noticed that he was trying to skirt around any remembrance of what happened. My friend who helped me go back into the house after my husband's death helped me walk through the pain, and I was able to eventually start coming out the other side. On the other hand, my friend's movement through life seemed to be constricted by his desire to avoid his pain.

I realized that when we avoid going through the scary stuff to face our pain, we carry it with us instead, and it influences how we navigate our life. When we go through it, we learn from it, we face it, we feel it, and we start to redeem the broken parts. In some cultures, they encourage a dramatic display of emotions by the aggrieved, but in America, we try to get through mourning with as little incident as possible, hardly acknowledging the loss. This is not just true of grief and loss; it is also true of all kinds of suffering. We tend to want to skip the face-to-face part of the journey that gives meaning and resolution to the participant.

YOU CAN'T RUSH HEALING

As we begin to dive into the more painful parts of trauma and the impacts it has on us, it is important to reframe the healing process. In our culture, we tend to rush through painful experiences to the other side, often just focusing on and talking about the positives. However, our approach is not the only way, and it is not necessarily the best way either.

When my husband died, I tried to move past it. I went back to school after the funeral. I didn't want to sit around at home missing him and making myself miserable, and I thought I could escape the memories at school. I heard "It will be okay" from well-meaning friends. And although there were moments I felt okay, there were times I wished I had died too. When one of my friends tried to reassure me, I had to be honest. "You are correct. It will be okay, but it's not okay right now. So if you are unable to sit with me while it is not okay, then I should probably let you go." This response might sound harsh, but when you're grieving, you can only take "It will be okay" so many times.

The truth is that most of us are so uncomfortable sitting with others in their pain and grief that we unwittingly rush them through it, invalidating their pain and ultimately causing them shame about their grieving. The underlying message we receive is, "If you could just see that everything is going to be okay, you would be happier and stop grieving. And if you can't, well, that's a failure on your part."

We celebrate others' ability to master their feelings in suffering. We expect them to have the "perfect" response, even though there is no perfect response. In my case, my colleagues appeared uncomfortable if something made me cry, but they seemed just as uncomfortable when I laughed (I assume because they thought it was too soon). It was as if I was just supposed to be neutral so no one else would feel uncomfortable.

Part of me wished that everyone I encountered knew my husband had died in our bed and then gave me compassionate responses, grace, and some leeway. In some countries, that's exactly how it goes. Americans tend to view suffering in a negative way. But in Haiti, individuals who lose a loved one wear black for three to four months, though the time frame is not set in stone. In cultures like this, those grieving are encouraged to honor their own process, and the grieving is not hidden away. In some cultures, people wear white to show they are in mourning. The color doesn't matter as much as the intention to honor mourning and give it space and acknowledgment.

Imagine if we were to do the same for individuals who had suffered a trauma. What difference would that make in a person's healing and ability to honestly address the impacts and move forward—if there was no shame in doing so?

In his Daily Meditation email I subscribe to, Richard Rohr wrote on October 17, 2018, "If only we could see...wounds as *the way through,*...then they would become sacred wounds rather than scars to deny, disguise, or project onto others... Healing is a long journey."

THE RIGHT RESPONSE FOR YOU

It is with this in mind that we take the next step into the impacts trauma has had for you. We can all read lists of symptoms and disorders that tend to result from traumatic experiences when "ACEs are high." But what really matters is the impact your trauma has had on you. This is not a one-and-done exercise either. It takes time to uncover the early trauma you experienced, the strategies you employed that may have literally saved your life as a child, and how unhealthy patterns have shown up in your relationships and life.

In late 2020, I was trying to be more aware of what triggers me and the impact of the triggers. One day, I received an email telling me why I needed to do something that I didn't believe I should do. When I read it, my anxiety went through the roof. It almost took my breath away. I realized I had been triggered by the email. The email in and of itself wasn't a big deal, but I felt like I needed to respond immediately and that my choice was being taken away. I felt like I had to do what the person suggested, and I was upset because I didn't believe it was the right course of action. Finally, I used my rational brain again and wondered, *Why do I think I have to respond immediately and do what is recommended?* I realized that my extreme reaction connected back to being invalidated as a child and being told to ignore the danger and take care of my mother.

It was completely rational that I was afraid of my mother.

She had a history of hurting people (me, my dad, my sister) and not just emotionally but physically. I was literally afraid for our lives! But my father often implied I was making more out of it than it was. It wasn't as bad as I thought. He minimized things because he didn't want to believe how bad it was. At one point, he even said that I was "lucky because I was my mom's favorite...Imagine what it was like for your sister." So when the psychologist told my father that I was in terrible shape, terrified of my mother, and would have emotional problems for the rest of my life, he was shocked. How could that be? I was the favorite. He was certain I had it easy! I eventually pieced things together. My father also saw his brother as their parents' favorite. He assumed his brother had life easier, and he applied the same reasoning when looking at me.

Only I didn't have it easier. I felt responsible to protect the family from my mother's terrifying and destructive rage. However, since I looked up to my father so much and he told me that I was misinterpreting things, I leaned into the very thing that terrified me and disregarded what I felt. I ignored the loud and clear (and, now I know, reasonable) concerns, disregarded my own safety, and got closer to and took care of the enemy.

I learned not to listen to my instincts that told me to run and hide and instead befriended and showed love and compassion to the very person who caused me terror. Eventually, I grew to believe that I made too big a deal of what was happening, so I could not trust my instincts. In fact, I grew to believe that when I was upset by something, I needed to look on the bright side and consider what was going on with the other person rather than look inward and determine what was impacting me and what I needed. After all, anytime I expressed sadness or anger, my mother would just laugh at me.

As I brought my attention back to the email, I realized all of that was coming up. Instead of simply reading the email and thinking, *That's not going to happen,* I felt terror. My fight-or-flight reflex was triggered, and I could literally feel my adrenaline rushing through my body. Why? Because my body was responding as if I was a young child encountering danger. I was that small child again encountering my mother, large and dark and full of rage. I was defenseless, and it was my job to calm the monster and make everything better so that she did not hurt people.

COPING STRATEGIES

As you consider the many and varied impacts trauma can have on a person and the many possible responses, it is time to consider the specific impacts and responses for you. My sisters and I all developed our own coping strategies and were all impacted differently, even though we had the same mother.

You may already have a strong handle on how you've been impacted by trauma, or you may be just starting off trying to figure out what the impacts are. Either way, remember the importance of grace before delving further into the impacts. It's the impacts of my trauma, more so than the trauma itself, that prompt feelings of shame. As a result, I encourage you to be diligent in exercising GRACE every day and maybe more when needed as you do the work to heal. Finally, remember that even if some in our culture don't have a gracious and loving response for you, your suffering is still real and important to acknowledge and resolve.

Take a moment to consider a few questions:

- Consider a time that you had an upsetting interaction as a child. How did you respond?
- In what ways do you react that helped you survive as a child but are unhealthy now? Did you scream and yell? Did you get quiet and try to appease? Did you run to your room and hide?

Whatever you did, you likely still do that today when your anxiety and stress go up. So if you yelled and screamed, you may find you fall into anger quickly. If you were quiet and tried to appease, you likely still try to make sure others are okay and attempt to ease their frustrations, taking little notice of what you need. Ask the following set of questions to yourself:

- Do I respond to some situations in a way that frustrates me? In my case, I would beat myself up maliciously when I made a mistake. The rational side of my brain would tell me, "This isn't that big of a deal," and yet I would ruminate on the mistake, telling myself what a horrible person I was.
- How has abuse impacted me? Do I minimize my feelings or experiences? Do I feel like I have to justify myself to others when they don't seem to understand? Do I feel like I have to have others endorse my decisions to feel good about them?
- Are there things that I do that set me up for more abusive relationships? Do I take responsibility to find a solution when someone else is in the wrong or make excuses for them?
- What messages do I notice running through my head that don't help me? Do I tell myself I should get over this or that? Do I tell myself I'm too sensitive? Inadequate? Unworthy?
- Do I neglect myself? Not exercise? Eat unhealthy foods? Neglect going to the dentist? Spend time alone feeling lonely? Avoid asking for help when I need it or decline help that is offered because "I can do it myself"?
- Do I criticize myself when I'm going through a rough time?
- Do I focus on scarcity rather than abundance (what I don't have rather than what I do, or a fear there isn't enough to go around)?

Regardless of the specifics of your experience, you undoubtedly developed means of coping. Behaviors arose that helped protect you from the full intensity of the situation. Likely, you had several strategies at the ready. As mentioned, many individuals who have suffered trauma have experienced some form of dissociation. If that is true for you, you've likely experienced losing track of time, feeling disconnected or separate from yourself, or even not feeling real.

My response was to attune to my mom and disconnect from what I felt. I had to respond quickly and know what upset her. If I considered or expressed what I felt or needed, that would provoke the most terrifying of reactions, so I had to detach from that and focus on her. As a child, my response made things far calmer in the household. And my mother saw me as her little savior, brightening her day.

As an adult, this meant I was disconnected from my feelings and needs and didn't clearly communicate either in relationships. My default answer was yes, and the idea of saying no shook me inside, making me feel I'd cause psychological harm to others if I set boundaries. So when I did say no, I usually wasn't saying it; I was yelling it or at least saying it with great intensity because it was only when I was angry that I could take that risk. As soon as my anger subsided, I found myself apologizing and trying to make up for my outburst, ultimately losing sight of the underlying need that was exposed. There were certainly better ways to express my feelings and needs, but instead, I chose to return to hiding. That felt safer.

If you're still struggling to determine how you've been affected, I'm going to walk through some common impacts of trauma, and you can assess whether any resonate for you. If they do, simply put a check in the box.

☐ Say yes when I want to say no to avoid conflict or avoid disappointing someone I love
☐ Distance myself from others
☐ Don't trust others or only share things that are historical or positive
☐ Erupt in anger at times that don't make sense or have other feelings that seem out of alignment with the situation at hand
☐ Lose track of time or am not fully present around others
☐ See myself as inadequate or unworthy
☐ Use or abuse substances
☐ Cut or harm myself
☐ Contemplate suicide
☐ Eat too much or too little
☐ Avoid crying or see it as a sign of weakness
☐ Compare myself to others
☐ Avoid being vulnerable and sharing my weaknesses or mistakes
☐ Don't know what I need or how to express it
☐ Avoid asking for help

- ☐ Believe I can handle everything on my own and don't need anyone or that I shouldn't need anyone even when I feel like I do
- ☐ Avoid conflict
- ☐ Struggle to know or articulate what I need
- ☐ Find myself drifting away, and others ask me if I was even listening

When you identify the coping strategies you have utilized, it is important to understand what purpose the strategy serves. It may seem odd to say that abusing substances serves a purpose, but it does. If it did not, it would not be so common in individuals who have a history of trauma. For example, someone who tended to dissociate as a child may find it harder to do so as an adult and therefore turn to substances to help alter awareness. Cutting, likewise, can create a euphoria or a sense of control that helps interrupt the psychological pain. A client of mine once said, "When I was being abused, I didn't feel in control of my body, so I cut when I am triggered to remind me I do have control." Some turn to overeating to feel unattractive and less enticing to a rapist; they believe this response will save them from another attack.

When you understand the reason behind each coping strategy, you develop a respect for it. You can't just get rid of something that has helped you survive without addressing the underlying pain or fear. To imply that a person will one day wake up and decide they won't use their coping strategy anymore is unreasonable. And yet, many of us feel guilty for the behavior. In no way am I suggesting you continue to cause yourself harm, but what I am suggesting is that it's critical to first respect the reason for it before looking for alternative responses.

So whatever coping strategy you used and still use today, no matter how shameful it may seem, it is important to recognize that it is there because it was an important tool for you. **It is not there because you are defective. It is there because you are adaptive**. And it has served its purpose well.

By reviewing the impacts of trauma and responses you've had, you will take away a list of strategies you've employed that no longer work in your life and are now causing more problems. The acknowledgment of the strategies and the awareness of how they have served you will become the foundation on which you rebuild your life. You will know where to focus by understanding why you developed certain strategies in the first place.

ACKNOWLEDGE THE PROCESS

The last thing I wanted was for my life to be dictated by my trauma, and so my tendency was to diminish and normalize anything I noticed. I tried to focus on my strength and grit and ability to deal with whatever arose. I went to see a counselor off and on to learn about myself and try to ensure I was taking care of myself and being as good a mom and spouse as I could. Because I'd been seeing a counselor off and on since around 1990, I believed I knew myself fairly well and understood my strengths and weaknesses.

Around 2004, I took a Birkman assessment at work, and it said that I didn't like change. I couldn't believe it. I thought I embraced change. It also showed that when I was stressed, I was harder on myself and less organized and able to perform. It has taken a lifetime to understand the impacts of trauma on my personality traits and address them. And knowing isn't always a sufficient motivation to do something about it. When I realized I didn't like change, it's not like I immediately started liking change. However, I did start being more compassionate toward myself when I was facing changes. I also made every effort to be kinder to myself when I was under stress—to slow down and make a list of things I needed to do to help me stay organized.

This assessment in 2004 wasn't my last wake-up call. I've had to continue learning about ways I've coped and patterns I've formed. Don't be surprised if you discover new effects of your abuse or don't notice something now and do later. Or if you notice the same impact repeatedly. This is all a process. And remember, you need time for play and rest too. You don't have to be constantly digging into your challenges.

At this point, it will be helpful to identify five to seven impacts that cause you the most trouble today. You can either jot down whatever comes to your mind first, or you can do so by going back through the questions and lists in this chapter. Prioritize the ones you most want to address as you move to the following chapters.

Although suffering is inevitable and will come into everyone's life at some point, you are not designed to suffer. You are designed "to shine, as children do." You were "born to make manifest the glory of God that is within" you.[11] If you do not believe in God, simply know you were created to manifest your innate ability to survive and live a meaningful life.

MY JOURNEY UNFOLDING THROUGH MY JOURNALS

Much of my life has involved new insights and newly refreshed insights (those insights that I had before but came into greater clarity as time went on). In many ways, my "journey of insight" began when I was twenty years old. By this time, I had become fearful I too had a mental illness. I wrote the following in my journal.

---

11   Marianne Williamson, author of *A Return to Love: Reflections on the Principles of "A Course in Miracles."*

August 1990:

I am going to see a psychiatrist and try to get some guidance.
It scares me. Lately, I've just become deeply depressed out of
the blue and gotten in moods where I take everything person-
ally and I just feel worthless, and I feel like driving off a cliff
and no one can change the way I feel. I feel like I can't control
my feelings or my level of stress. I just want help.

I went to a psychiatrist who said I did not have mental illness.
However, she said I was very angry with my mother. I had
no idea how she could tell and wondered, *Is it that obvious?*
She gave me a referral to a counselor, who I'd end up seeing
for years.

At age twenty-three, I realized how much I did not like confrontation. I was deeply concerned about others' reactions
to me. I avoided confrontation as much as I could.

When I was twenty-four years old, I started taking psychology classes to prepare to apply for graduate school in
marriage and family therapy. These classes brought me face-
to-face with a lot. I began having violent dreams in which I
was powerless, afraid, and being pursued. During this time,
my mother often called wanting me to take care of her emotionally. I was beginning to deal with my anger at the abuse,
but I still didn't remember much of what had happened to
me. It was mostly fragmented memories.

In my journals, I tried to figure out how to navigate healing.

October 1994:

I feel strongly there is more, and I feel safe that I will never remember it. I never thought I'd say that, but I feel safe not remembering and I don't know if I can ever completely heal without the memories...I like to think I can.

At age twenty-five, I saw I was clearly challenged in understanding and expressing what I needed. My husband was struggling with his own challenges, and I was desperate, exhausted, and angry. I believed myself to be responsible for others' behavior and was often consumed with shame. I began to notice particular thoughts that would trigger a feeling of shame.

I also realized how much I focused on disappointments and others' rejection of me. I finally began to see this focus wasn't helping. So I turned my attention to the progress I had made in addressing my difficulties and the forward momentum.

Still, I was afraid of loneliness and uncomfortable being alone. When I found my husband dead in our bed at age twenty-five, I didn't know how I was going to move forward.

November 1995:

I have to slow down, breathe deeply, and open my senses to what my mind and body are communicating to me. What am I feeling? What am I needing? What or who are safe places? In what ways can I get my needs met? Who cannot meet my needs? Where or with whom do I feel safe?...I'm feeling pain, anger, shame, fear, loneliness, guilt, and no joy...In the meantime, I need to learn how to nurture myself, love myself, accept myself, and trust myself.

CHAPTER 5

BE THE PHOENIX
AND RISE

*"It's better to take many small steps in the right direction than
to make a great leap forward only to stumble backward."*

—CHINESE PROVERB

Now it's time to build out of the wreckage and reestablish
hope by choosing one area to address—one area to impact.

When I was twenty-three years old, my mom called me and
said, "I had a dream about you. You were two years old, and
you were my savior." I don't remember what she said after
that because I sat there stunned, thinking, *Wow, that is really
messed up and is going to make great content for many counseling sessions.* And even though I knew her view of me was
unhealthy, I had no idea how much it had impacted me. I

laughed at the thought of me being her savior at two years old, and at the same time I grieved how much her view of me wreaked havoc on my life.

It wasn't until around age forty, while I was sitting in church, that I felt I could finally release the burden of being a savior. It was as though God was saying to me, "I love you. You've done a good job, and you don't have to be a savior anymore." I remembered what my mother had said nearly twenty years prior and realized I was still playing the role of savior. I still felt responsible to make sure everyone around me was okay. If others were upset, I disconnected from myself and did everything I could to relieve them. I realized that until I let go of the savior persona, I would never be able to fully trust and let others in, and ultimately, I would never be able to heal.

So after church, I walked to the back where the prayer team members were standing and asked for prayer—to stop playing the savior. I was so overjoyed when I left the church that day until I realized a harsh reality: if I wasn't a "savior," I wasn't really sure who I was. I spent the next couple of years figuring that out.

I had to learn how I was still playing the role of savior in my life and where I could get better at connecting with what I needed and making those needs known. I had to be reborn with a new identity and learn how my new persona would manifest. What would I do differently?

Soon enough, I realized that I needed to let others in, share more vulnerably, and let others help me. And that was terrifying! What if I didn't look like I had it all together? When I shared openly, would they think, *Well, of course she became a clinician. Clinicians are just trying to work their own stuff out.* I would be so ashamed if they knew how broken I felt. Changing how I showed up would require an entire makeover; it would likely be a lifelong project. But if I didn't try, I would always be a "savior." No matter how big my fear, my desire to be healthy was stronger.

Being a savior required me to embody many maladaptive approaches to engaging with others. For instance, I would:

- Only share things that were historical and that I had already "successfully" navigated.
- Stay away from expressing vulnerability, such as not crying or talking about fears
- Disconnect from others before they disconnected from me
- Act as if nothing upset me, even to myself
- Work endless hours and always feel like it wasn't enough
- Disconnect from what I needed
- Not express my needs
- Anticipate others' needs
- Always put others' needs first
- Rarely say no
- Attempt to always understand others' perspectives and consider them first (though I wasn't always successful)

- Only feel good about myself when I was helping others
- Require myself to always be able to find a solution or a positive perspective
- Feel responsible for others' negative emotions or responsible to make them feel better
- Put off saying no to someone until the last minute (unfortunately, this usually caused more problems)

Since I couldn't possibly change all of the ways I showed up as a savior at once, I had to focus on one part at a time and trust the rest would follow in time. Step one for me was to exercise more trust in people in my life who were trustworthy—more specifically, to share what plagued me. I knew how to complain to others, but I wasn't as practiced in exposing my real fears and opening my ears to what I could do differently. I had to become willing to share that I didn't have all the answers and allow others to inform my actions toward healing.

START SMALL

As you pivot from a list of coping strategies that no longer serve you, it is time to select one or two you would like to address. Dealing with our coping strategies and the impacts of trauma can be overwhelming and might feel like climbing Mount Everest or running a marathon. It is important to take it one step at a time.

Take some time to consider where you will start. What do you want to address and improve? Avoid trying to resolve everything at once. Keep this in mind: addressing one thing impacts everything, and addressing everything is overwhelming and will only make you want to give up before you get started. I've lost count of how many people would come to the workout class I attended at the beginning of a new year and be gone by March. When I joined the class, I had been working out for years and slowly built to that point. For many, this was their first class, and it's no wonder they grew frustrated and quit altogether.

With your new awareness and an incremental focus, you might think you should just be able to flip a switch and wake up healed. But that's not a realistic expectation. Instead, you want to approach the healing journey like a phoenix.

The phoenix is known for being reduced to ashes and then emerging and rising from what was destroyed more capable than ever. It is important to note, however, that the phoenix doesn't rise as an adult but as a fledgling (a baby with new wings ready to leave the nest). It is such a good illustration of starting small in your ascent rather than expecting to rise as a whole person, claiming victory over everything that has plagued you. A fledgling can typically only hop, flop, and maybe flutter, but it doesn't start off in the majestic ascent. In fact, the mother bird is nearby to protect the fledgling in its early learning. Similarly, it can be very helpful for you to have support as you begin to reclaim yourself.

When starting small, it is important to consider momentum. It's not about hitting a home run the first time up but about stepping up to the plate. You will never hit a home run if you don't step up to the plate. I don't play baseball or softball, and yet this makes sense to me. There are many small steps leading up to every success. And without each step, success cannot be achieved.

We often expect ourselves to take all the required steps and claim victory the first time. When you are contemplating healing from trauma, you may think, *Well, I should just be able to do this or that because it's logical and just good sense.* And so you pile the list high when trying to make changes. However, any new behaviors require practice and result in increments of progress. The operative word is "new."

As you consider the impacts of trauma on you and the coping mechanisms you've created, you now have the foundation on which to RISE...

RECOGNIZE	Make a list of what you want to improve.
INVESTIGATE	Find possible solutions.
SELECT	Pick a few of the solutions you will try.
EXECUTE	Try the solutions.

You will not RISE once but again and again. Understand this is **a process, not a destination**. That said, you can also be confident it is a process that will get you to your desired destination.

No one would expect an infant to come out of the womb and walk out of the hospital at discharge. That would be absurd enough to be recorded by every major news publication. A baby must first sit, then crawl, then stand, and then walk. Sometimes a baby will skip a step, but there are always steps between birth and walking that we have come to accept, which is why new parents don't force the issue with infants or become frustrated that their newborn isn't walking when they first come home. Likewise, you should extend yourself the same grace.

Change will come incrementally, not all at once. Every step is an achievement, even when you flounder, because that's when you learn the most. Sharon Salzberg says in a meditation, "When you notice your mind has drifted or you've fallen asleep, with great kindness toward yourself, begin again, because this is the time when you have a chance to be really different." I love that because it reminds me that when I notice a blunder, I have a chance to change how I respond. This is important to remember as you begin. Rather than focusing on the failure, I focus on the opportunity to choose a new way to be.

WHERE TO BEGIN

As you determine where you should begin, here are some questions to consider:

- What do I most want to improve?
- As I look at the impacts of my trauma, where do I want to intervene?
- What is bothering me the most, or what do I find most triggering?
- What seems to steal my joy?

Answering more positive questions might point out something you want to increase:

- What brings me joy?
- When do I feel safest?

I encourage you to consider what area of your life you would like to be different and healthier. In order to heal more intentionally, you have to figure out what you want to improve. This one area is likely made up of lots of parts and pieces. Take some time to write down all the parts and pieces, as I did earlier in the chapter. Once you have established a list, find one or two things that grab your attention to address.

As you move forward, keep in mind that you may change your mind about the ultimate destination. By taking small steps, you have time for learning and adjusting on the journey.

If you are finding it particularly difficult to figure out where to focus, here are some further suggestions that can get you started. Consider:

- Areas where you neglect or abuse yourself
  - Unhealthy eating
  - Negative self-talk
  - Self-injury
- Times you struggle to ask for help or show vulnerability
- Ways you are hard on yourself
- Patterns of staying in unhealthy friendships or intimate relationships
- Where you have poor boundaries
- Situations in which you're reactive

The goal is to clearly identify one area to focus your attention. You will learn a lot as you continue your journey, and you can always shift your attention as needed. The most important part of the exercise is to be intentional, no matter what your focus is. The more you contemplate the impacts and narrow your focus down to one primary area, the clearer everything will become.

"Habit is habit and not to be flung out the window by any man, but coaxed downstairs a step at a time."

—MARK TWAIN

In 2009, I had an encounter that made me realize I had clung to a "savior" persona that was not serving me, and I began to intentionally move through my own pain and fear to hope and healing.

I still found myself playing savior. I had taken great pride in being a "breadwinner," in being tough, in having insight (or at least thinking I had insight), and yet being a savior was like having a noose around my neck. It was keeping me from truly healing. This identity lifted me up with accolades, and it oppressed me with its weight. It was deceptive in its allure, making me feel special, while at the same time making me feel worthless and disdainful.

June 2009:

The role (savior) had created bars for me that kept me trapped in a world of extremes.

The extremes that jailed me were as follows:

- *Superior – inferior*
- *Judgment of others – self-hatred*
- *Arrogance – insecurity*
- *Blaming others – blaming myself*
- *Blame – shame*
- *Perfection – failure*

August 2009:

Today is killing me, but I continue to try to meet the demands that are placed on me no matter if they are insurmountable (and right now, my work demands combined with all that I have going on with my private practice, church, and my four children is too much)...

The underlying message my mother gave me was, "You are my savior. You are so special; you are able to make all things better. If you don't, you aren't doing your job and you have failed. You are a worthless human being."

December 2009:

The last couple of weeks have been very difficult. I have been really angry, reactive, and generally sensitive. Today, I broke down. I have effectively dismantled or at least begun to dismantle the "savior" complex and it has been my identity and purpose all my life. Now I have no identity and purpose. Without work and at home on vacation, I have nothing holding me together. It's like removing a skeleton from a person's body; it can't stand. My purpose has been holding others up, making others okay emotionally.

What do I want my identity and purpose to be?

In 2010, I began leaning into my faith and trying to release defensiveness and pride. I wrote of addressing issues rather than reacting. I was still placing a lot of pressure on myself to always consider others' feelings, and I still seemed to have no apparent awareness of the need for boundaries. If something went wrong, I tended to think it was probably my fault. Or as I used to say, if it was 10 percent my fault and 90 percent someone else's, I focused on my 10 percent and beat myself up relentlessly.

In this time, I also realized I had slowly given up all the things that brought joy to my life, such as singing, whistling, going to church, and hiking, and had increasingly been either at work or at home.

January 2010:

I signed up to share my story with my church in a small group on January 27, 2010. I expressed my fear regarding sharing "my story" as it involves abuse and I fear being discredited as a therapist. I assumed people would think my history is what caused me to become a therapist. I wept and felt a great deal of shame. It was as if I could physically feel dirt all over me. I wanted to disappear.

February 2010:

I met with the original prayer team...We prayed about my child-hood and abuse. And one of the women asked me to think of God being with me as we prayed. As I did, it was if I saw God sitting next to me, under the table as I hid, whispering to me, "I will bring you through this," and that was exactly what was happening.

In early 2012, I began to explore my tendency to overextend myself. It seemed much of my self-worth came from my work. I realized that I had been prioritizing work success over self-care.

March 2010:

I am so fulfilled in my job, I allow it to take priority at times. I work through needed potty breaks. I wake up most nights thinking about work and resolving problems.

So most recently, I allowed myself to get dehydrated because I simply didn't drink enough fluids. I knew it was happening, but I continued to neglect my needs. When signs of a UTI arose, I self-treated and tried to move on. It didn't work. I know there are a lot of things going awry in my body, which makes me wonder why I would allow this to happen. Self-care has to be the highest priority. After all, how will I succeed at anything if I don't take care of my body?

I feel depressed by the mess I live in, but I have no energy to do anything about it.

As the year progressed, I started taking better care of myself.

In late 2012, as I journaled one night, my breakthrough happened. For two years, I had been trying to figure out who I was if not a savior, and then it came to me.

October 2012:

Who are you to say that I am God? I was never God. I'm a person! A person! A person!

I realized that instead of being a savior, I was a person. Which meant, like other people, I had no supernatural ability to handle pain or help others, because I was human—fallible and vulnerable.

In my savior role, the lie was that I was special and was in a special role. Bullshit! I was being oppressed with unreasonable expectations and robbed of my humanity.

CHAPTER 6

DEFINE YOUR DESIRED DESTINATION

To get somewhere, you must first know where you are going by clearly defining your desired destination. The same is true when you are trying to change and grow; you must determine how you would like things to be before you chart your course.

When I was in junior high, my ability to dissociate was fading. I was starting to feel inadequate, and my friends were not being kind to me. My favorite teacher even accused me of stealing from her. It seemed like nothing was going my way. I spent a lot of time feeling depressed and alone. As I transitioned into high school, I was tired of being judged and caring what people thought of me. So I decided, in my teenage wisdom, it seemed like the best thing to do was to start using substances and use enough that I wouldn't feel. When my friends picked on me because I was a virgin, I took care of that too. I was angry and reactive and trying to send a message to the world that I was impenetrable. All along, inside, I felt completely alone.

When others drank, I drank more. I slept with boys and didn't care who they were. And I did drugs whenever they were available to me—fortunately, that wasn't very often. During that time, my friend's parents grounded me from their house. I was not allowed to come over or spend time with my best friend.

Just before my sixteenth birthday, I decided I didn't want to live like this anymore. I stopped having sex with boys and stopped drinking and using substances. I realized I didn't want to be a person who would sleep with my friend's boyfriend or spend my life running from myself. I wanted to heal.

Around this time, my father had introduced me to Alateen, a support group for teens who had parents with alcohol dependence. I started going to a twelve-step group, got a sponsor, and worked diligently on my steps. It wasn't perfect. In the twelve-step program, you're not supposed to get into a new relationship within the first year, and I was in quite a few or at least flirting with someone most of the time. Still,

I had a sense of who I wanted to be, and it included living honestly and addressing my issues head-on. I continued to date, but I refrained from physical intimacy, stayed sober, and worked my steps.

My desired destination was to have serenity, feel, and share honestly. I didn't know how my trauma had impacted me or even that it had. I just knew that I wanted to heal, and I knew I was holding on to a false persona by trying to ensure everyone thought I was tough and nothing impacted me. If I felt hurt, I reacted in anger to push others away. I knew none of this was working in my favor or getting me any closer to what I wanted. So I started to focus first on what I didn't want (the life I was living) and slowly unraveled the life I did want.

SPRINKLE SOME FAIRY DUST

One of my favorite techniques to help my clients get from point A to point B is to identify their desired goal by asking the "Miracle Question." This technique was created by Steve de Shazer, who provided solution-focused counseling.

The idea is to imagine that while you're sleeping, a fairy comes to you and sprinkles fairy dust over you, making the problem you want to solve go away. You don't know it's gone because you were sleeping when the miracle occurred. When you awake, how will you know the miracle has occurred?

More specifically, what will you do that you wouldn't usually do when you had the problem, and what will you stop doing that you would usually do?

Consider these questions for yourself and begin to write out your responses. What is the first thing you will notice when you awaken? Be as specific as you can. As you write out what will be different, you are defining your destination. Make sure you consider what you will be "doing" differently and not just differences in what you will feel.

Once you have detailed the destination, you will better understand what you need to start doing and stop doing. This is a good time to figure out where you want to start.

Here is an example. Let's say the problem you decide to address is poor boundaries or "people pleasing" behaviors. While you are sleeping, unbeknownst to you, a fairy comes and sprinkles magical dust on you and a miracle occurs: you now have healthy boundaries. When you awake, how will you know you now have healthy boundaries? Maybe you feel stronger and more confident. What will you be *doing* differently because you feel stronger? What will you not do that you usually do?

The answer could be that you will not always say yes but instead consider whether you want to do what is requested, and you will say no if you don't want to do it. If you say no and the person persists, you will persist with your no or remove yourself from the situation entirely.

As you continue the exercise, you might think, *I also won't feel guilty when I say no.* With continued questioning, you will explore how you will know you no longer feel guilty by what you will be ***doing***. Maybe you will know you don't feel guilty because you won't question your decision and ruminate about how it impacted the other person.

All of this provides you information about what you need to start doing more (e.g., saying no sometimes) and start doing less (e.g., giving in to every request). As you put the learning into practice, you'll need to stay with your no and not compromise it when pressed. You'll replace the self-doubt with positive affirmations, such as "I'm so proud of myself for saying no because even when it was uncomfortable to do, I did it and didn't compromise. This will keep me from feeling resentful." In time, you will find that others respond to the new way you have chosen to be. They will accept your no as no and will not persist in trying to get you to say yes.

CREATE YOUR MIRACLE

Now it's time for you to take the problem you selected in Chapter 5 and create a miracle. Be as specific as you can be about what you will be *doing*. How do you know the miracle has occurred? Make as long of a list as you can of behaviors that are evidence of the miracle that happened as you slept.

If the miracle question didn't get you to a desired outcome, another approach you can take is to consider times that things did work as you wanted. If you cannot remember such a time, start making note of experiences you have where you feel or behave as you would like to. Make note of what you are doing when you feel that way. For instance, using the boundary example, are there times you set a boundary and feel okay about it? If so, is it with a particular person? What makes the situation different from when you are not able to do so? How do you make the boundary?

Don't just think about it. Write down the specifics from your miracle or the great and glorious times where things worked as you would like them to all the time. Be as detailed as possible and specify what you will be doing or not doing that punctuates the miracle or difference. Remember, you can't get to where you want to be if you don't know where you want to go.

If you didn't get this impression yet, being specific about what you would be specifically **doing** or **not doing** is important, because it will translate to your list of what to do and not do.

Try this to frame out your future.

MIRACLE: Imagine a miracle happened last night as you were sleeping, and the problem you selected in Chapter 5 has been taken away and is no longer there. When you awaken, what is the first difference you will notice that will indicate a miracle has occurred? What will you be doing or thinking that you don't usually do or think?

....

....

What will you *stop* doing or thinking that you usually do or think?

....

....

BEST TIMES: At what points in your life have you felt the opposite of your problem? For example, if not trusting is your problem, at what point did you trust someone?

....

....

What were the details surrounding the situation? What was happening? What was not happening? Who were you with?

What allowed you to trust (or another outcome) in that particular time? What were you doing that made your desired outcome clear?

....

....

MY JOURNEY UNFOLDING THROUGH MY JOURNALS

After a very challenging season in which so many things were happening at work and with family that I could not change, I spent months trying to figure out what I needed to do to improve things. Try as I might, the challenges were what they were. I spent time making gratitude lists and grieving the losses, and finally I started to focus on what I could control.

October 2020:

I'm entering into a season of abundance, not by circumstance, but by intention. With a belief that what you focus on expands, I am shifting my focus to all that is happening that is life-giving rather than the alternative.

CHAPTER 7

CREATE A PLAN

"A goal without a plan is just a wish."

—ANTOINE DE SAINT-EXUPÉRY

"The most important step a man can take. It's not the first one, is it?

It's the next one. Always the next step, Dalinar."

—BRANDON SANDERSON, *OATHBRINGER*

Now that you know where you want to go, you will need to develop a plan or roadmap to get you to your desired outcome. Going on a trip without a map is like turning off the lights and trying to find a particular shirt in the closet; it leaves you grappling in the dark. You don't have to plan the entire journey, but you do need to be able to see the next step.

One of my clinical supervisors in graduate school used to say, "When a person says, 'If I've told you once, I've told you a thousand times,' your response should be, 'If you've told them a thousand times and a thousand times it didn't work, maybe it's time to try something different.'"

I realized just how true this was when my son continued to fail classes, and I continued to become more and more restrictive in my approach. First, he was required to sit at the dining room table and do schoolwork for thirty minutes each day, then an hour, and then two hours. I'm sure you know where I'm going with this. The result stayed the same. Only now, the tension between us had grown.

My daughter would come home with straight As, and I would smile and say, "Good job," and quickly move on to focus on my son. Then one day, I remembered my professor's words and thought, *Hmm, I think I'll try something else. I will just do the exact opposite of what I've been doing.* And so, I turned everything upside down. I told my son he didn't need to sit at the table and could choose not to try if he so desired, and if he failed, he would pay for summer school, but really it was up to him to decide whether or not he was going to do the work.

I also started rewarding the effort put in. I told my children that for straight As they would get $20, and for As and Bs they would get $10, and anything else would not get a reward. When I gave $20 to my daughter, $10 to my younger son, and nothing to my eldest son, my youngest inquired, "What about Roderick? What does he get?" I said, "Well, Roderick didn't get As or As and Bs, so he doesn't get anything." Roderick then smiled at me, knowingly.

I don't think it was the money that made the difference, but I do think taking the exact opposite approach to the situation put the responsibility squarely in his court. I was no longer pressuring him or trying to force the issue; I was giving him space to figure out what he wanted. And apparently, when I got out of the way, he wanted to pass his classes. He graduated in the top eleventh percentile of his class.

SHIFTING THE FOCUS

As humans, we have a tendency to notice or focus on what is not working rather than what is. We become experts at describing the problem and are ill-equipped to describe the solution. I was completely oriented around failing grades and spent little time acknowledging passing grades. Even though I should have acknowledged Bella's effort more, I gave a cursory "Yes, dear, good job," and I was off as quick as a wink to Roderick.

We focus on the times things are not going our way and all the details surrounding it, and we oftentimes talk about it repeatedly in frustration. When things do work, we don't tend to give it the same attention. Therefore, we don't know the details surrounding the success. The simple truth is that what we focus on tends to expand. So if we want more of the successes, it will help to drill into those more and understand the nuances involved when things go well so we can be more intentional.

We started to shift the focus in Chapter 6 as you concentrated on your chosen aim. Now it is time to determine the first step or two you will take to start moving toward it. How you start doesn't matter as much as picking somewhere to start and getting started. Or as Nike likes to say, "Just do it."

My approach to doing parenting differently with Roderick had nothing to do with finding a proven method of parenting and everything to do with making a 180-degree change in how I was approaching the situation. I had three basic beliefs that fueled the change:

1. What I was doing was not working.
2. Continuing to do it would produce more of the same.
3. I had nothing to lose by trying something starkly different. So I just considered what the opposite approach would be to what I was doing and tried it.

There are many ways you can establish your approach to solving the problem you have selected. You can do any of the following to create your plan:

- Start with what you're already doing that seems to be working and do more of it. This means making note of any times things are going the way you want them to go and be specific.
- Do the exact opposite to what you have been doing. Again, be specific about what exactly you typically do or do not do now and what an opposite approach would look like.
- Jot down ideas of things you have wanted to try but haven't yet.
- Research approaches others have used to address the same problem, and pick a couple that sound good to you. This could include writing down a detailed account of how someone else handles comparable situations in a manner that you admire.
- Try different approaches to see what works for you. If you struggle with anxiety, you could try meditation. For busy minds, guided meditation is a wonderful place to start. If you want help figuring out the impacts of your trauma, you could start receiving counseling from a trauma-informed therapist. If you want to address connected health issues, consider changing your diet, exercising, and resting more, or seeing a practitioner to address the specific concerns that ail you.

When you consider the next step, clearly describe what you will do and ensure it is fairly easy to achieve. If you start with something that is extremely challenging and you don't meet your own expectations, you are likely to give up and not try again, believing you are flawed in some way or incapable.

A PLANNING FRAMEWORK

I created a Practical Planning Framework to assist you in determining your next step in the process. It is important to assess the degree of difficulty the new behavior will involve. You will have more success by starting with easier items, and as you get going, the more challenging ones should become easier too. As you go, it is helpful to keep track of opportunities to incorporate new behaviors.

Example Practical Planning Framework:

PROBLEM:	MIRACLE:	CHALLENGE LEVEL:
What I want to stop doing	What I'd do if a miracle happened 180° change in behavior	1 (easy) to 10 (hard)
Being unsure what I need or want	Be clearer on what I want or need from any given situation	5
Saying yes when I want to say no	Say no when I want to say no	4
Saying yes when a person persists in asking after I say no	Stick with my first answer	7
Beating myself up for saying no when I was able to do what was requested	Praise myself for making a boundary even though it was hard	5
Telling myself it is rude to say no	Tell myself it is good to say no because it keeps me from expecting others to know what I need without me asking	5

Your Practical Planning Framework:

Take a moment to create your own Practical Planning Framework using the example. Once you have completed your framework, you are ready to take action. Part of your plan may involve seeking help for healing through clinical intervention. If the Practical Planning Framework doesn't help, then just make sure you jot down what you will try that is new and different.

MY JOURNEY UNFOLDING THROUGH MY JOURNALS

In this series of journal entries, I began to identify the issues I wanted to address and how I'd address them.

In 2015, I was having difficulty erecting boundaries. I felt like doing so was rude. I believed it was not okay to say no, and I was concerned about how I would be perceived if I did. I wanted to be validated by others, but instead, I sometimes felt others took me for granted. It took me time to realize I expected them to make boundaries for me and was upset when they failed to do so. I saw others' "lack of appreciation" as the problem, rather than my inability to establish boundaries.

I also realized I tended to run when I was wrong or embarrassed. I wanted to leave before I was rejected because I felt so inadequate and unworthy. I realized I would need to be vulnerable and real to get different results.

So I started to do the things I knew were good for me even when I didn't want to do them. For instance, I journaled even if I didn't feel like it. I exercised when I felt like sitting on the couch. It wasn't easy. I'd see others run by me on the trail pushing strollers. One person was using sign language, pushing a stroller, and still running faster than me. At times, I certainly felt discouraged, but I kept showing up and stopped expecting myself to be great at things right away. Instead, I counted showing up as success.

I realized I put the bar so high for myself I could not succeed. And when I fell short, I beat myself up maliciously. I didn't even notice the progress I had made. So I began to cycle away from self-criticism, a focus on scarcity (on what wasn't rather than what was), and thoughts of my shortcomings, and *toward* acknowledging what I had done and believing I could do anything if I took things one step at a time.

August 2015:

I struggle a lot with self-critique when I'm under stress. When I need grace the most, I give myself the least.

What I want to believe about myself—

What would it be like to let go of the extremes and understand everything likely falls somewhere in the middle? You're not the best or the worst...you are you. Not better than or less than, just right...right where you are. You are fallible and imperfect, which makes you relatable. What you give is enough. Who you are is enough. You are sufficient. Not better or worse. Making a mistake doesn't make you a failure; it makes you human.

December 2017:

I'm starting a mission to diminish the comparing I do. It is my goal to understand the purpose it has served, acknowledge it, and release it.

...Now I use comparison to understand others, to be okay, and to figure out that for which I should strive. I would think things like, "She's smarter than me" or "I would never do that."

In this time, I began to look to others' behaviors only to validate who I was or know who I wanted to be (or not be). I started to embrace who I was and accept that not every characteristic of mine is a flaw or reaction to something awful but sometimes simply part of my nature.

When I was better at accepting myself, I made more room for those I love to express their hurt and frustration without internalizing it or thinking their words meant I failed. I realized I am not to blame for everyone else's negative experiences and feelings. And once my response wasn't only focused on me, I could actually see and be there for them.

December 2017 continued:

The other person wonders why you can't just listen to them and hear them. They know what they are sharing isn't about you. They don't see you as a failure but rather as a resource, a companion. And so, in that dynamic, the trust is compromised, and it is more challenging to connect.

The dynamic reinforced my belief that the world is unsafe. So I decided to stop thinking everything someone said or did was about me and started assuming everything someone else did was the direct result of something going on with them. After all, I didn't expect others to be responsible for my feelings, and I wasn't so unique as I had once thought.

This process of taking steps toward my goal was *so* liberating. I had grown up carrying the burden of others' pain. This mechanism protected me, but it also alienated me. It eroded trust and made it harder for me to truly connect. I was responding to other people's feelings through confrontation rather than seeing an opportunity to exercise trust and vulnerability.

CHAPTER 8

"JUST DO IT"

"You miss 100 percent of the shots you don't take."

—WAYNE GRETZKY

Gretzky was also quoted as saying, "Maybe it wasn't talent the Lord gave me—maybe it was the passion." The reason Gretzky was known for the shots he took was because he took so many, and he took so many because he was passionately dedicated to improving.

"Take action! An inch of movement will bring you closer to your goals than a mile of intention."

—STEVE MARABOLI

When I was sixteen years old, I decided to take a tennis class at the local athletic center. I was so excited. I had always wanted to play tennis and had never taken any lessons. As the day approached, my enthusiasm grew. By the time I arrived, I had butterflies in my stomach. I was finally doing it. I was going to be a tennis player, and I couldn't have been more excited.

I went out on the court with my racket in hand and quickly noticed that everyone else in the class was nine years old. Don't get me wrong; we were all on the same skill level. I was just two feet taller. The coach gave us instructions, breaking down every movement by the basics. The instruction was perfect for where I was, but I was so humiliated that I decided my first class would be my last class. My ego could not take the bash that came with my tennis peers being half my age, so I quit pursuing the thing I had been so thrilled to do!

It took a while for me to go back to tennis—a long while. At thirty-four years old, after my mother and father had passed, I began treating myself to sweet frozen coffee drinks and maple pancake sausage sandwiches on a regular basis. Before I knew it, I had gained twenty pounds. I realized it might be time to do something that was life-giving rather than trying to soothe through instant gratification. So I decided I would try tennis again. I would push through the imperfect and likely uncoordinated times to finally achieve my long-term goal.

I flipped the pursuit of immediate satisfaction on its head by committing to something longer lasting and good for me.

I had to commit, knowing I'd quit if I didn't dedicate myself to trying long enough to improve. I hated thinking of how much work it would take, but I was committed.

So I went out week after week. This time, at least my peers were my age. The first few times, I think the other players were irritated, wondering if I'd ever hit a ball near them. After all, they were also there to work on their game, which, unlike me, they actually had. In time, however, I started learning where to be and how to hit the ball. Then I learned how to serve the ball. Before I knew it, a group invited me to join a tennis league. I wondered if they knew how bad my tennis game was, but they seemed to think it was good enough.

And after a couple of years, I was winning games and perfecting my placement and speed. But it wasn't about how many games I won. It really never was. It was about what I was claiming for myself. I came out of that experience with a new skill, a lesson about the benefits that can come from showing up ready to learn, and a great group of friends.

James Clear, in his book *Atomic Habits*, talks about starting small and building from there. We began that process in the last chapter by identifying one thing to change, something easy enough that we could improve our success rate.

With incremental steps forward, you will learn not only

what works and leads to success but also what does not work and leads to failure. Like anything, your approach will need to adapt over time. Inventors know this well. Edison tried 3,000 designs for a cheaper light bulb before landing on one, according to a Live Science publication (article "Who Invented the Light Bulb?"). In every meaningful process, failure leads to progress and reaching your ultimate goal. It's the nature of trying new things. As we start moving from plan to action, it's critical that you not allow failure to be an obstacle in your progress.

Nelson Mandela said it best: "The greatest glory in living lies not in never falling, but in rising every time we fall." When we fail, we learn what doesn't work. This process can be even more informative than succeeding.

There are many popular examples of the importance of failure. After Steve Jobs was fired from his own company, he used that experience to reconsider where he was going. When he returned, he transformed Apple. (You may be reading or listening to this right now on an Apple device.) Charlize Theron saw her mother kill her father but kept putting one foot in front of the other. Oprah Winfrey was fired as a television reporter and then started her OWN television network. Not only did she suffer rejection, but she has a documented history of molestation and miscarried at age fourteen. She was able to take her pain and transform it into inspiration. She didn't let rejection stop her progress.

Many well-known people suffer from post-traumatic stress disorder and continue onward. They have boldly shared with others their suffering and rising. The list includes Ariana Grande, Whoopi Goldberg, Barbara Streisand, and Lady Gaga.

KEEP GOING

Dispel any thoughts that you cannot rise. The only way forward is by taking action to heal—no matter how small the steps may seem, even if you fail in your first attempts. As mentioned earlier, your suffering has not disqualified you. Instead, it has equipped you with sober understanding that life is imperfect and suffering is inevitable. Your persistence is evidence that you are ready to rise.

There are some things you can do to make the beginning easier. Here are a few ideas:

- **Get started NOW.** Don't start tomorrow or next week; start today. Even if what you are doing today seems small, if it's taking you in the direction of your goal, do it.
- **Make small efforts and repeat.** If you make small efforts many times, you produce momentum that fuels your progress.
- **Find a friend.** Find someone to serve as an accountability partner to you. The person needs to be someone who is supportive of you and is there to encourage you,

not criticize you when you make mistakes or drift into old behavior. Most of us are experts at pointing out our own missteps and failures and don't need help there. It's really helpful to have a friend who is trying to accomplish something similar and maybe has you as an accountability partner too.

- **Make it measurable.** You need to be able to tell if you have succeeded, and you also need to make sure you're using the right measuring stick. For instance, I started doing an aerobic workout three times a week after reading that scientists had found a connection between aerobic activity and improvement in the brain of individuals with MS. My measurement of success was that I got up and went three times a week, not how hard I worked out or whether I lost weight. It was important to ensure that that was my focus.
- **Celebrate every success.** Celebrate every time you do what you set out to do. For instance, congratulate yourself every time you establish a boundary, no matter how it felt or how well you did. Trust you will get better with practice. Better yet, celebrate every effort!
- **Learn from mistakes.** Take mistakes as opportunities to learn. Mistakes often teach a person more than success. So embrace the *whole* journey, not just the positive parts.
- **Give it time.** According to the Huffington Post, "on average it takes more than two months before a new behavior becomes automatic...sixty-six days to be exact." That

means the first couple of months are an exercise in will. Consider the following process:

- ◦ Apply action to your intention. You framed out what you are going to do, and at first, you are going to just do it regardless of what your brain is telling you.
- ◦ Apply intention to action. The benefits you notice in time will inspire a deeper desire that makes not doing it less appealing than doing it.
- ◦ Just be. This is when you can stop thinking about your plan and just live it out. The actions become an integral part of you and your routine.

- **Apply what you know**. Take in what sets you up for success. You are the expert on you. I work out in the morning because I know as the day continues, my excuses grow, and by the end of the workday I tell myself, "I'll do it tomorrow." Since I know I'm less likely to do my workout the later in the day it gets, I've learned I need to work out first thing in the morning. What have you learned about yourself? How will you apply your learning?

Whatever you do, don't let what has happened interfere with you persevering toward what is ahead. Don't allow your weariness in the journey dictate your dedication to the cause, because the cause is *you*. As you journey, the landscape will change and your perspective will too. Trust that even if you have not yet realized the wonderful accomplishments you desire from your efforts, you will. So whatever you do, go, take risks, try things. Take needed time to rest along the way, but never stop.

MY JOURNEY UNFOLDING THROUGH MY JOURNALS

January 2013:

I don't want to be avoidant, but I also know I don't have to put myself knowingly in painful situations that don't add to the greater good. I need help discerning one situation from another.

At this point in my journey, I realized I had been unwittingly engaging in situations that were painful to me. And I decided to start investing in life-giving endeavors instead. I began a more intentional relationship with "my person." I came to an understanding that as a person, I wanted a relationship with someone who was my equal, someone I didn't need to save...two people forging a path side by side.

I began to let go of the past, and my anger began to lessen. I started to strike more balance between work and life. I was no longer working twelve hours a day and actually took a full day off each weekend. I was also beginning to love myself a little.

February 2013:

The last couple of days I've begun feeling bad for claiming joy for myself. Why does my joy matter?

...I grew to believe I was broken and somehow also a savior, and

now I know neither are true! I am a person—imperfect and divinely loved.

...I have begun to learn what it is to be a person...allowing others to know my vulnerabilities, learning of them myself. This transformation has been scary but freeing. I have shed thousands of tears, tears of sadness and of joy. I have learned what it is to trust. I have learned to recognize trustworthy behaviors in others. I have left my isolation on my island, and I am no longer alone. It makes me feel alive.

It's like seeing for the first time—full of hope and questions, curiosity and fear, vulnerability and joy. The discovery is unending. I realize the negative messages I was told about being disgusting were crap!

In 2016, I noticed I had difficulty sitting with the unknown and tried to control the journey and outcome all the time. I often had painful reminders that inspired me to action. I found that a restlessness for more tended to push me through pain and uncertainty to new places. I had a month off work between jobs that gave me time to contemplate all that I had neglected in my life and create a plan.

In April 2016, I decided to do what I could to invest in my well-being more actively.

- I was having fatigue during the summertime from my

multiple sclerosis (MS), and I weighed more than I wanted to. So I did Whole30.

- I realized I was spending entirely too much unproductive time in thought. So I started meditating more regularly—a few days a week rather than intermittently.
- I wanted to address my fatigue in any way possible. I had read an article that indicated more aerobic exercise had been associated with remyelination of the brain. So I increased my exercise from three times a week to five and specifically started doing weights two to three times per week and aerobic exercise three times a week.

By October 2016, I had:

- Lessened my mental chatter and decreased ruminating on negative thoughts and fears
- Lost twenty pounds
- Connected to my feelings
- Diminished my reactions to others' feelings
- Lessened fatigue in the summer from MS

CHAPTER 9

INCREMENTS OF INSIGHT

"We do not learn from experience...we learn from reflecting on experience."

—JOHN DEWEY

Insights come incrementally over time. We tend to learn the same thing repeatedly, gaining deeper understanding, insight, and healing each time. Even if what you try does not result in the outcome you envisioned, it is still good. As long as you contemplate what happened, you will learn from it and your next attempt will be more effective. Now that you have tried some things, it is time to reflect and adapt your approach.

Early on in my career, I was invited to the Walton Leadership

Institute for a leadership training of their District Managers. About halfway through the training, they had everyone at the training leave their tables and gather around a mat on the floor. The mat was square, about twenty feet by twenty feet, and looked like a large checkerboard. They told us we were not allowed to speak during the activity and each person got only one shot. The object to the activity was to get from one side of the board to the other without making the buzzer go off.

The first person started by taking a step onto the mat. Nothing happened. We breathed a sigh of relief in unison. As the person took one more step to the left, "BUZZ." We all jumped. Everyone made a mental note: the fourth white checker over has a buzzer, and we have to make sure no one else steps on it. We gathered around as the next person stepped on the same first checker and we all frantically gestured where not to step. Then she stepped to the right checker. Nothing happened. Again, everyone took a breath. She stepped forward toward the other side. "BUZZ!"

This went on, until finally one of the participants was able to make it across. As she stepped on the last checker, the room exploded with cheers. We had done it. We figured out the path. What was most notable was that the missteps had taught us as much as the right steps. It was just as important to know where *not* to go as it was to know where to go. The errors were teachers and just as necessary. And rather than thinking of them as bad, we saw them as information.

Even though you may want to complain and lament your mistakes, you should also learn from them. If you notice immense anxiety or anger erupt at a situation that doesn't seem to warrant it, ask yourself, *What is it that triggered me?* Then look at what your response was to the trigger. What has helped you deal with the trigger and the resulting response? For instance, when I realized an email triggered me and I felt like I had to respond immediately and concede, I did the opposite. I did some deep breathing and took a moment to consider my response, and I didn't respond until later.

The anxiety and anger are like an emotional "BUZZ," indicating you need to try another direction. To go the other way and not step on the part of the checkerboard that buzzed for you, you must first understand what happened to create the reaction. You can't avoid something if you don't know what it is.

Likewise, when you try something and it doesn't work, consider what exactly didn't work. Was it a complete failure? Did some aspects not work while others did?

MY INCREMENTAL INSIGHTS

Throughout the book, I've shared excerpts from my journal to show you what this healing journey might look like in practice. In this chapter, I will share even more from my journal to illustrate how insight comes over time. As you read more about my experience, consider how much you have already learned, and know that you have much more to learn as you continue taking steps forward, one at a time.

This is where you apply a kind of twelve-step "take what you like and leave the rest" approach to your journey. Some of the things you have tried will have helped you advance your miracle, and others likely left you disappointed.

In my mid-twenties, I began to recognize how the issues I had as a child were the same I experienced as an adult. I think at some point, I thought I would resolve these issues and identify new ones to address, but I never fully resolved the core issues because to do so would have required uncovering my triggers, vulnerabilities, reactions, and problematic approaches.

This recognition allowed me to reform my approach. I increasingly asked the question, *How has that response served me in the past?* I stopped intentionally responding in unhealthy ways, but I still repeated unhealthy patterns I had developed to cope. Now, at least, I was beginning to see what I did unintentionally too.

In 1997, at age twenty-seven, I realized I often talked a lot to try to talk the painful things out of existence. I also had little to no boundaries when it came to sharing personal information with others.

I don't like it when I share personal things with people I hardly know! And yet I do it all the time! How can I start trusting myself more if I always look to others for comfort and answers rather than being still? I know that as a child and an adult, I have been known to try to "talk" painful feelings away rather than sitting with them; however, sitting with feelings is much less embarrassing...Why do I insist on everyone validating me?

Since it made me feel bad when I shared personal content with people I didn't know all too well, I changed my approach to sharing. I saved the most private elements of my life for my closest friends. As I made this change, I noticed I felt less concerned about my disclosures.

In 2004, at age thirty-three, when I lost my father, I reflected on his repeated requests for me to come and see him for Thanksgiving the previous year. I had already taken time off from work to be at my mother's bedside, and I thought it was too much to ask. As was my tendency, I didn't ask work if I could take more time to see my father over the holidays.

My mother's funeral was the last place I saw my father. I beat myself up about that too, telling myself I should have gone to see him. I felt awful I wasn't there for him. I only needed to learn this lesson once; I would never again prioritize work over family. The BUZZ was loud and clear. My priorities were off.

In 2013, it had been thirty years since I started keeping a journal. Sure, I had typed up some thoughts on my father's computer earlier, but actually keeping track of my thoughts, desires, challenges, hopes, and so much more started in 1983.

August 2013, age forty-three:

Almost thirty years later. I'm finally in a relationship where I am heard, respected, seen, and honored, and I am learning how to honor myself.

There is a lot of wreckage from the past...I tell myself that all I can do is pick things up from today and move forward. Today is all I have.

In 2014, I started dealing with my feelings more—not just anger and happiness but sadness and shame. In turn, I became more aware of the times I was disconnected.

March 2018, age forty-seven:

I'm noticing when I'm being self-critical. I'm catching myself with negative thoughts...I'm reacting to things I don't like in myself with things like, "Get over it!"

I noticed I was swinging from extreme to extreme, positive to negative, like my mother did in her commentary..."You're my savior" to "You're disgusting. I can't believe anyone would marry you." I either felt amazing or worthless. And it wasn't my mom's commentary anymore. She'd been gone for nearly fourteen years; it was the critic inside my head.

I'm trying to reflect on Sharon's words of recognizing I've stepped off the path, and with great kindness toward myself, I begin again.

2019, ages forty-eight to forty-nine:

I discovered I had more strength than I thought to deal with the most challenging of situations. There were times I wanted to shrink, but I was steadfast. At this time, I began erecting healthier boundaries while maintaining fulfilling relationships, something I had not yet done successfully.

In January, I started off my year with a question: *For what are you willing to sacrifice your joy?*

In November, I wrote: *These past few weeks have been incredibly stressful, and I am trying to increasingly embody the serenity prayer—letting go of the things I cannot control and using my energy to address things I can influence.*

By December, I was realizing exactly what I needed to do to have healthy boundaries: *I realize I've felt responsible to make everything better...Holding on to something I cannot control only creates anxiety and spin for me. It takes me off focusing on how I can care for and be gentle with myself and erect boundaries for myself and use my voice. I have spent so much of my life minimizing my own pain and feelings and keeping my anger to myself...*

In 2020, just before my fiftieth birthday, I was going through a very stressful situation and my friends were starting to become worried. I was filled with anxiety and my head was on overdrive. Day and night, I tried to figure out how to deal with the challenges in my life, and my hope and joy were dwindling to almost nothing.

I had been trying to focus on things that I could control and let go of those things that I could not, but try as I might, my anxiety was rising. I began meditating daily and went back to my counselor for support. After a few weeks, I realized I needed to invest intentionally again in things that gave me life. So I began to work in my off hours on preparations to write this book. It took my focus off what I could not control and breathed life back into myself as I leaned into what I believed to be my purpose.

In a nutshell, I shook the cobwebs off my dreams and brought meaning back into my life. Overthinking and analyzing had been stealing my joy and disconnecting me from those around me, leaving me hopeless and disheartened. Very soon, the tone of my counseling sessions went from hopelessness and a focus on dire circumstances to hope, meaning, and genuine excitement about the possibilities. I was spending time creating, rather than replaying my despair.

Each time I have gone through something challenging, I have gained deeper insights and risen even more. This most recent season gave me the greatest healing. I found that even when life is at its darkest, I can find joy and hope.

January 2021:

I'm trying to focus on my own behaviors that contribute to unproductive or unhealthy dynamics. I realize I, more than anything else, feel responsible to fix things that cause others pain. I am uncomfortable with asserting boundaries that cause others sadness, etc. Then when feelings erupt, I've been known to try to talk them away or make it better. So I'm trying to figure out what I need, learn how to ask for what I need, and to more easily, without taking anything personally, respect others' boundaries.

For me, boundaries feel like rejection. For me, boundaries feel selfish. I realize Henry Cloud is right that boundaries are necessary like property lines. Boundaries are information about territory.

In the year of writing this book, I am still learning. The insights are still coming. In February of this year, I wrote:

In the meantime, I will lean into that which brings love and light and enables me to live my purpose. And I will take my focus off that which is dark and distracts—and release all of that.

A STORY WITH MANY CHAPTERS

Our lives are full of challenges and blessings. As we go, we learn. In my story, I had to learn to face painful experiences and move through them. I had to confront the things that terrified me the most, sometimes with my eyes squeezed tightly and other times with my eyes wide open. I had to boldly feel into the depths of myself. All in all, I have been resolved to rise, to become a better version of myself, and to claim my own destiny and not the destiny that seemed unavoidable.

What is your story? Have you also found that you are learning the same lesson again and again and finding new ways to address it? What I can guarantee you is that if you continue to bravely pursue the very best this life has to offer, you will achieve it.

Along the way, it's critical to reflect and change your approach as needed. For example, I had to see that my behavior communicated that others' thoughts and feelings mattered and mine didn't. I thought I was being generous and self-sacrificing, but I was doing everyone a disservice. In the end, I felt angry and spent entirely too much time lamenting my situation—time I could have spent enjoying my friends within healthy boundaries. It was as if I was getting angry that others don't help with dishes without ever asking for help. I was expecting others to know what I needed without me knowing or telling them. I was neither taking care of myself nor helping others know what I needed.

My story is not perfect. Far from it! But it is earnest and full of endless possibilities, just like yours. And the possibilities are coming to fruition because I am committed to always pick myself up after I fall and do the best I can to learn from the experience. In no way am I saying I won't feel sorry for myself at times or stay down for a few minutes just to acknowledge the difficulty, but I will always rise eventually.

"The one who falls and gets up is stronger than the one who never tried. Do not fear failure but rather fear not trying."

—ROY T. BENNETT, *THE LIGHT IN THE HEART*

Are you in relentless pursuit of something better? If you are, then every time you fall, dust yourself off, determine what caused the fall, and explore a different route. What are your other options? Read books, listen to podcasts, ask questions, stay curious, be bold, and always remember to be compassionate toward yourself. It will never be perfect.

What is the greatest learning you have taken from your journey? Maybe you, like I, have kept a journal or otherwise documented your quest. If so, the pivotal moments along the way, the moments that propelled you forward or advanced your efforts the most, will rise off the pages and greet you. Or maybe you have made mental notes as significant events have occurred in your life, which remain highlighted in your subconscious. Either way, determine why those specific moments were so impactful, and you may find the key to unlocking your next discovery.

Take a moment to jot down your BUZZ moments and the moments when everything flowed and worked. By doing so, you will know how to navigate around what doesn't work and focus on what does.

CHAPTER 10

GUMPTION AND GRIT

It is time to recalibrate and rise again. You now have greater insight and more commitment as momentum propels you forward. You can go back to the beginning and find new areas to address or address the same areas with innovative approaches. Sometimes, you will return by choice, and other times, situations will prompt a return to the start.

I had to return to many core wounds in late 2002, when my mom's husband had found a new love and left her after twenty-five years of marriage. She was depressed and struggling with emphysema and cirrhosis of the liver. She went to the hospital periodically to have the fluid drained from her lungs, where she met a terminally ill man and developed a relationship. They would sit and receive their treatments together and keep each other entertained.

Unfortunately, my mother's new boyfriend died in 2003, and her mental health plummeted into the ground. For the first time in a very long time, she stopped taking her medications as prescribed. And her symptoms began to reemerge. Around June 2003, she called me. "Lilli," she said, "I might be the second coming. Or you might be the second coming." Sadly, I laughed off her delusional state and was happy to take a breather from talking to my mom for a while.

During my breather, in September 2003, my mom lost all clarity and was so disorganized she could not communicate. My youngest sister saw the decline and made sure she was admitted to the hospital. As my mom began to clear, she started talking about her dogs and her Avon lady. She was still incontinent, but things were improving. Then she urinated, slipped in her urine, and cracked her skull.

I received a call from my sister that our mother was in the hospital after a fall and not expected to make it. When we hung up the phone, I purchased my airfare and flew out the next day.

At that point, I realized the poor timing of my break from our conversations—a decision I regretted. Now I was at her bedside, and I was incredibly surprised that at age thirty-three the first thought that flashed through my mind when I saw my mother in her weakened state was, *You can never hurt me again.* Up to that moment, I had no idea I was still concerned she could hurt me. I was a grown woman with three children, afraid my mother would hurt me. The thought stunned me.

I didn't understand why, at that age, I would still be afraid of my mother. When witnessing her last breaths, it seemed a more suitable thought would have been something like, *Oh my gosh!* or *Oh shit!* When I gazed at her and saw she had left her body, I breathed a sigh of relief because I was finally safe. The experience would certainly serve as a point of conversation with my therapist when I returned.

I had spent years in counseling. I had unearthed challenges, faced them head-on, and attempted to work through them. And on that day, I realized there was more work to do to address my fear. As you live, information presents itself all the time. Sometimes you notice the same exact pattern. Other times you notice a similar pattern from a new perspective or a pattern you never before recognized.

My life has been a slow and steady journey of rising and falling and rising again. I have always desired to be better, healthier, and more fulfilled than I was, and as a result, I have always sought after healing and growth. None of us are perfect, and no solution we attempt will solve every issue we have. But with slow and steady effort and renewed focus and learning from the journey, we can create momentum and ascend out of suffering.

BACK TO BASE CAMP

Did you know that to reach the highest peaks in the world, a climber has to repeatedly go backward to base camp? They hike up to the first point and then go back to base camp. Now that they are acclimated to the first height, they now go up to the second point, only to return to base camp again. They do this until they are looking at the peak. Yet they still have to go all the way back to base camp before they can touch the peak.

During this process, the body is adapting to the altitude and lack of oxygen. Similarly, when you reach an important point of healing in your journey, it is not time to skip off down the road. It's time to go back to where you started, reflect, and prepare to reach an even higher point. As you return to the list you made in Chapter 4 and again contemplate the impacts of your abuse, you can do so with a new understanding and hopefully greater self-compassion. Oftentimes, we think that moving backward from our ultimate destination is negative and a distraction from the goal, when it is actually a necessary part of the journey.

Alison Levine, a mountaineer and the captain of the first ever female American Everest expedition, reminded me of this as I sat and listened to her speak at a corporate training. She says, "Every time you get to the base of a mountain (literal or metaphorical), you're presented with a new opportunity to challenge yourself, to push your limits beyond what you thought possible, to learn from climbers on the trail ahead of you, and to take in some amazing views. Your performance on the mountain you climbed last week or last month or last year doesn't matter—because it's all about what you are doing right now."[12]

REVIEW WHERE YOU'VE BEEN TO MOVE FORWARD

My encouragement to you is to go back to base camp, metaphorically speaking. Go back through the process I've outlined in this book whenever you feel stuck. Remember how far you've come. And then keep going!

An important part of returning is noting that everyone suffers—suffering is universal (Chapter 1). It's also important to remember that trauma, in particular, can cause lifelong challenges to the person experiencing it (Chapter 2). With these realities in mind, you can reground yourself in GRACE (Chapter 3) before you examine how trauma has impacted you and make a list of what you want to address (Chapters 4 and 5).

Another important reason to go back is to notice whether your final destination changed. If so, how do you reach that miracle? This is time to consider what new behaviors you will manifest (Chapter 6).

After you figure out where you are going, you must decide

---

12 Alison Levine, *On the Edge: The Art of High-Impact Leadership.*

where you will start (Chapter 7). What will you do that you haven't been doing or stop doing that you have done? As you get going, practice moving step by step (Chapter 8); do something new or stop doing something. Remember that some things will work marvelously, and others won't work at all in getting you where you want to be.

Keep an eye out for what works (they're the keepers) and discard what doesn't work as you continue forward. You will learn as you go (Chapter 9). You will face discouragement and setbacks along the way, but keep going. You're worth it!

MY JOURNEY UNFOLDING THROUGH MY JOURNALS

I realized that no matter how many times I thought I had learned a lesson, I continued to go back to my old, familiar behaviors that didn't work. Here are some journal excerpts during that time.

April 11, 2015:

Surrender, leaving the temple, leaving home...All involve leaving what is known for what is unknown. All involve a departure from what feels safe and familiar for what is risky. Our departures are from various things, people, behaviors, depending on what crossroad we find ourselves. If we don't depart, we eventually end up in a cyclical trek back to where we started and around again. If we are willing to be vulnerable, not have the exact roadmap, and need others, we grow and end up someplace new with new possibilities. Otherwise, it's more of the same, and like still waters, we become stagnant.

So where do I find myself? In similar behaviors reaping predictable rewards with the same consequences. The stress is familiar, the ego attachment the same, and I find myself connected to and justifying where I am.

May 4, 2015:

The last trek around the well-traveled path is more painful than all the others! With new insight that it's time to move on, the final hours are permeated with clarity and repeated echoes in my mind: "Why did you need to do this again?" And my answer, "Because it took a little more pain and sacrifice to realize there was no benefit being reaped." For me, it's about knowing I don't need to prove myself anymore. Departing this chapter isn't the failure I had perceived it to be but rather a victory.

It's me claiming myself. I've learned everything this particular experience has to teach me. If I'm completely honest, I will admit I don't like change. It is wrought with undiscovered territory. What if I fail? At least the behaviors I'm in are known. Is that solace enough? It isn't anymore!

So in the midst of the journey and around to the next off-ramp,

I'm preparing myself. I'm learning to trust my instincts and celebrate the newly found honesty I've secured. It's painful, but it's real, and moreover, it's the right next chapter. I'll grow because I haven't memorized the next path.

What is familiar is comfortable, like an old blanket or an old pair of shoes. And who doesn't like comfort now and again? The problem is when we stay stuck in what's familiar, even though it isn't healthy or healing. When a climber climbs, they have moments of leaving what is known for what is unknown so they can reach new heights. That is what you are doing. When you return to the beginning and take another honest look, you are taking a moment to sort through the brokenness and pull out the pertinent pieces of your experiences and your responses so you can investigate why they're there and what you would like there instead. As you consider what you want and envision the future through a new lens, you are starting your ascent once again with greater clarity and a deeper commitment to the trek.

Sometimes you will have to go back to move forward. It's all progress. When you have resolved yourself to rise regardless of your circumstances, you are in the long game. You are not centered on immediate gratification but steady and persistent efforts to achieve your goal. And as the saying goes, "Slow and steady wins the race." Sometimes a simple step backward will be the exact thing you need to progress toward your goal.

CHAPTER 11

IN CLOSING

As I prepared to write this book, I pulled out more than forty years of journals from various nooks and crannies of my house. One by one, I stacked them up in a pile. Then I pulled them out and put them in chronological order from age thirteen to the present; there were thirty of them, and several were still missing.

I read all of them from beginning to end, seeing more clearly the course I took from suffering to rising. I went back to the beginning—well, at least as far back as was available for me to go—and jotted down the themes emerging in each journal.

At age thirteen, like many other girls, I was boy crazy; I talked about boys incessantly. I was clearly seeking out a sense of okay-ness. I didn't feel worthy of gifts, and I didn't like myself much. Slowly but surely, I started to talk in my journals about finding happiness and healing and finding my own love for myself separate from others' approval. And then I started reading entry after entry where I was telling myself I needed to be better, do better—not considering that I needed something. Each sentence echoed in my head. And I felt angry. It was all the messages I grew up with, but this time it wasn't someone else saying them. It was me. I had internalized the messages of invalidation and disdain and continued to replay them.

I set the journals down and took a break for a few days because I was being reactive. I was snapping at my family and replaying old tapes about what I should have, could have, or would have done. I was reading my shame scripts. During this process, I determined to get help to identify my needs, establish boundaries, and start taking better care of myself.

I had been reading books on the topic and was ready to find someone who could help me make this trek. As I researched, I ran across a YouTube interview with a clinician who spoke about boundaries. She specializes in epigenetics and works with people on inherited family trauma and its impact in the body. Everything she said resonated with me, and I found out she was available for virtual counseling. I emailed her and got the ball rolling.

In our first appointment, I went all the way back to the beginning. I talked about growing up, my mom, my dad, my parenting, and my subsequent relationships in adulthood. She quickly noticed how I talked about my experiences and my resulting thought processes and gave me powerful insights. She wove the insights into a meditation in which I could deal with my trauma and become aware of its impact in my body. In this way, I could find release from it. She also made a meditation for me on boundaries.

I had made inroads with all my efforts over the years— expanding my awareness of what thoughts and behaviors no longer served me—and yet I still carried the trauma from so long ago in my body. I still struggled at times with erecting boundaries with those I loved. And through just a few sessions, I learned a bit more about myself, learned how my triggers could be felt and resolved in my body, and began connecting with a new inner dialogue centered around me taking care of me. Since then, I have faithfully listened to meditations each time I notice I am again being more reactive than compassionate, and I have noticed my awareness increase.

The truth is that I will be learning and healing as long as I am alive. We all will, in one way or another. I imagine this most recent return to my base camp will not be the last. In fact, I already have in mind another journey back I need to take— to two early nicknames I was given: Clowney and Monkey. We were forbidden from laughing at the dinner table, a rule I often broke, and my father recounted the many times he found me climbing everything in sight. The next return to my base camp will be to retrieve more of the playful and vibrant person I was born to be. My focus has often been on extinguishing problematic areas of my life and less about discovering more goodness.

In this next part of the journey, I will take some time to list out what brings joy to my life and make every effort to increase it. What will be the next part of your journey? Have you discovered parts of yourself you want to know more about and will explore? Or maybe you have made a decision to stop doing something that no longer serves you.

MIRACLES ALONG THE WAY

You are going to get out of this life what you put into it. You will face discouragement, but you will also know encouragement, hope, and even joy.

I've shared stories with you of suffering abuse, having my husband die in bed next to me, being diagnosed with autoimmune diseases, and losing both parents within months of each other. Sometimes life has felt intolerable, but I've always found even more reasons to celebrate. My many friendships, people who sat with me in my darkest hours, a stranger in the car ahead of me buying my Starbucks, opportunities to share my story in front of thousands of people at work, a spouse who partners with me in mind, body, spirit, and so much more. It's important to reflect on the glory of this life whenever you can, even in the midst of hardship.

I've experienced countless miracles and blessings along the way. Each one made my life a little lighter and easier to navigate. Sometimes the bright spots came through individuals who cared for me.

As a young girl, I had Aunt Debbie. My sister and I stayed with her during the most tumultuous time in our lives. She took us out for hikes in the forest to collect pinecones and other things from the woods. We would then return to her home and work on arts and crafts. It was a deep reprieve from my sorrow and terror. She also gave me a model of what mothering could look like—nurturing and loving. As a teenager, Linda, my neighbor across the street, took an interest in me and treated me as if I were her daughter. She was forgiving when I made mistakes and also modeled loving and engaged parenting.

Sometimes my hope was advanced by what I considered miraculous experiences.

When I went for my first infusion treatment after my MS diagnosis, I met some of the kindest people. They encouraged me even though they were there for something far worse. At work, I met people who opened doors for me in the corporate world and gave me opportunities to prove myself. I had the privilege of sharing in others' journeys as they faced their fears and found renewed hope and inspiration.

The evening after Todd died, I was in our bedroom with my daughter Bella, my sister, and a friend of mine. Bella was one and a half years old. She was a buoyant being, full of life and joy, with a smile that seemed permanently planted on her face. I was exhausted and sitting on the bed with my back against the pillows. Bella sat on the other side of the bed near the corner. My friend stood in the corner, across from the bed, chatting with me as I processed the events of the day.

Suddenly, Todd walked into the room (in spirit) and went around the bed to Bella. I had spent years with Todd and knew him. It was the oddest thing, like his essence walked into the room in the same shape and form as his body. Bella stood up and raised her hands in the air to him. "Daddy, Daddy," she said as she gestured for him to pick her up as he had a thousand other times. I could sense he was conveying to her that he was in heaven and could no longer pick her up, and he loved her very much. He spoke to her without words as we think of them. She collapsed to the bed with her hands clasped around her face and wept. Even at one and a half years old, she seemed to understand the full breadth of what he was telling her.

After that, Todd came back around the bed to me. His joy was undeniable, and I'd never experienced him so incredibly enthusiastic. He communicated to me. "Lilli, I've been released from all my struggles." He let me know he was free. Later, he came back to show me how he traveled through light, and in so doing, each burden was stripped from him and his peace and celebration intensified. He had come face to face with God, and it was as if his brokenness was turned into crystal—pure and clear. He radiated immense joy. Then he said, "I'm so happy for you!" I conveyed to him I didn't understand why he would be happy for me as I was now a widow with two children and had no idea what I was going to do. He said, "I have seen your life, and you are going to do amazing things and bless so many people." Then he left.

On October 20, 1995 (nearly a month after his passing), I wrote in my journal: *I feel him come to me and smile over me, but our communication (his messages to me) are brief; each time he seems more spiritual.*

It was because of his visits that I had peace through the funeral preparations, the funeral, and the following months. Yes, I felt deep grief. At times, I even wanted to be dead with him, as I was terrified of being alone and raising the children by myself. But his visits to me and to others (who shared their experiences with me) supported me and made my healing more complete. His words of seeing my life and its significance have given me hope in some of my darkest hours.

What miracles or unexplainable circumstances have arisen

in your life that have made the heaviest of moments lighter? What people have served as encouragement or an example of how things can be? Or maybe during some of your hardest times, people came alongside you and showed you the way.

RECLAIM YOUR IDENTITY

One of the greatest learnings I've taken away from my life's journey thus far is that things can and will get better if you are willing to lean into every experience and hardship and learn from it. This is easier said than done. It is easier to complain and lament, but there is little gained from staying in that space.

In the past several years, as I've faced great blessings and hardships, I've grown more than ever before. I've realized my tendency to put self-care at the bottom of my priorities and have moved it up the list incrementally. In so doing, I now identify and erect boundaries, extend myself more grace, work out consistently, eat a fairly healthy diet without the foods that make me feel sick, meditate regularly, receive counseling as I need it, read books that inspire me with hope and equip me for greater healing and joy, and I even do a better job at staying hydrated. To this day, I still play tennis and enjoy wonderful and trusting relationships.

As you go through this journey and go back to reset and move forward, remember that growing is a process. You will realize more of what you need each step of the way. And perhaps even more importantly, you will be able to reclaim who you are. An intentional ascent to claim the true essence of who you are and want to be is an endeavor worth taking. When you have the courage to do the work, you will experience miracles.

Thank you for allowing me to take this part of your journey with you. I hope that from here, you are able to live your life as a person who has experienced trauma and not as a traumatized person. There is a big difference between having an experience and claiming an experience as your identity. You are not your trauma, and your identity is grounded in so much more because you have resolved to rise.

APPENDIX

The following are helpful resources for you in your journey.

TRAUMA THERAPY APPROACHES

There are many approaches to addressing trauma. Each evidence-based approach has been clinically proven to address the negative impacts of trauma. It's hard to figure out what therapeutic approach is best for you if you don't know anything about them, so here is an introduction.

Note: This is not an exhaustive list but gives you some idea as to what is out there. It is also important to see if you feel safe with the counselor. Remember, counseling is for you, not for the counselor. Your opinion and impressions are important. You cannot heal if you don't feel safe and don't trust your therapist.

APPROACH	UNDERLYING BELIEF	HOW IT WORKS
Dialectical Behavioral Therapy (DBT) Evidence-Based Treatment Approach	People are doing the best they can and want to improve but need to learn new behaviors and increase motivation.	A type of CBT that attempts to identify and address negative thinking patterns and aid individuals in living in the present. Teaches life skills.
Internal Family Systems (IFS) Evidence-Based Treatment Approach	The human mind is subdivided into an unknown number of parts, and that is a good thing. The parts contain important characteristics, and the self knows how to heal. There is no such thing as a bad part, and IFS looks to bring all parts into harmony. When trauma occurs, some of the parts (especially the self) go into exile, leaving the person unintegrated.	The therapist helps bring parts out of exile and hears about their fears and purpose to better understand and integrate. Therapist helps the client learn to trust the self again.
Eye Movement Desensitization and Reprocessing (EMDR) Evidence-Based Treatment Approach	Traumatic memories are stored in your body and brain, and flashbacks are an accurate reproduction of the traumatic event. Learning occurs when you create new mind and body associations with memories. This approach deals with trauma stored in the right hemisphere of the brain.	Helps you build bridges between the hemispheres while remembering the incident in small doses. Helps you develop feelings of safety, peace, and relaxation. The therapist creates what is called a dual awareness state using bilateral eye movements, a pulser, or tones that alternate sides.
Somatic Psychotherapy Somatic Experiencing (SE) Evidence-Based Treatment Approach	Trauma is experienced and held in the body, because there is a connection between mind and body. Healing must happen in both mind and body. Acknowledges that talk therapy isn't sufficient for healing.	Client tracks physical sensations and impulses in the body when talking about trauma or other stressors. SE therapists sometimes utilize touch, weights, movement, and visual techniques to help integrate trauma into the rest of the brain.
Trauma-Focused Cognitive Behavioral Therapy (TF-CBT) Evidence-Based Treatment Approach	CBT focuses on the relationship between thoughts, feelings, and behaviors and indicates that changes in one realm can improve how one is doing in the other realms. For example, changing a person's unhelpful thoughts can lead to more productive behaviors and improved emotional stability.	Therapy involves a child or adolescent impacted by trauma and their trusted caregiver or parent. Therapy includes psycho-education, development of healthy coping skills, processing thoughts about trauma and resulting beliefs, and may encourage clients to reconsider their patterns of thinking and assumptions.

APPROACH	UNDERLYING BELIEF	HOW IT WORKS
Prolonged Exposure (PE) Evidence-Based Treatment Approach	Most individuals who have suffered trauma want to avoid anything that reminds them of the event(s), but doing so makes things worse. Facing the fears can decrease symptoms of PTSD.	The client is encouraged to gradually deal with the trauma memories and associated feelings in an attempt to take the sting out of the memories and grow in the realization that the memory is not dangerous and therefore doesn't have to be warded off.
Gestalt Therapy	The whole is more than just the sum of its parts. Emotions and frustrations can be internalized and have an effect on your body. Healing happens through deeper understanding of oneself and the impact of the world around them.	Therapist works to determine what is getting in the way of the healthy process. Can include "empty chair" work, psychodrama, and graded experiments (doing instead of talking) to access past experiences more fully and bring the experience into the room to work through it.
Polyvagal	Evolution has endowed all humans with a continuum of innate defense behaviors that go from arousal, fight or flight, and then freeze or shutdown. Understanding the body's response makes us more in tune and compassionate. Acknowledges that shutdown happens in trauma and is not done voluntarily.	Look to see how client is responding and what state they are in (activated, fight/flight, shutdown). Clinician helps clients to feel safer and move out of the fight-or-flight or shutdown state. Client and clinician both are aware of their state, creating a connection between the nervous systems of each. Safe and Sound Protocol or integrative listening is a specific technique used.
Narrative Exposure Therapy (NET) Evidence-Based Treatment Approach	Focused on addressing individuals with multiple experiences of abuse. Believes that traumatic memories are encoded in a nonverbal part of the brain. Those memories are triggered by situational cues and are involuntary.	The therapist helps the client narrate all past abuses in chronological order into one story. The therapist creates a safe environment whereby the client reads the narrative and experiences the related emotions while staying present in the here-and-now.

A NON-EXHAUSTIVE LIST OF BOOKS THAT HAVE HELPED ME ON MY JOURNEY

The Body Keeps Score by Bessel van der Kolk, MD. Describes the physiological/neurological impacts of trauma.

In Sheep's Clothing by George K. Simon, MD. Describes the personality and behaviors of covert aggressive individuals and what makes a person vulnerable to that type of manipulation.

The Autoimmune Epidemic by Donna Jackson Nakazawa. Explores the many theories of the etiology of autoimmune disease and impacts of diet, environment, and much more.

Boundaries: When to Say Yes, How to Say No to Take Control of Your Life by Henry Cloud, MD, and John Townsend, MD. Shows how to develop healthy boundaries; written from a biblical framework.

Embraced by the Light by Betty Eadie. The most detailed account of a near-death experience that has given many individuals hope after the loss of a loved one.

Strategies to Empower Your Healing (8 Keys to Mental Health) by Babette Rothschild, MSW.

You Are the One You've Been Waiting For by Richard C. Schwartz.

10% Happier by Dan Harris. Talks about using meditation to elevate your mood.

The Four Agreements by Don Miguel Ruiz. Articulates simple truths that equip the reader with a path to freedom and peace.

The Shack by William P. Young. This book prompted my journey of transformation from "savior" to "person" and is a beautiful story of God's unending love and grace.

What Happened to You? Conversations on Trauma, Resilience, and Healing by Oprah Winfrey and Bruce Perry, MD. Oprah brings rich recollections of past abuses, and Dr. Perry applies the science to the changes to survivors of trauma. Most importantly, changes the question from *What's wrong with you?* to *What happened to you?*

ADDITIONAL RESOURCES

Somatic (Body) Work

- Work with the body can help significantly with dissociation.
- http://www.somatictraumatherapy.com/
- *Healing Trauma: Restoring the Wisdom of Your Body* by Peter A. Levine, PhD (an audio download on Sounds True)

- Somatic experiencing increases your understanding of why you react the way you do.

https://ifs-institute.com/practitioners - Find an internal family medicine practitioner in your area.

https://istss.org/home - International Society for Traumatic Stress Studies; provides information and resources to both clinicians and survivors.

https://www.nctsn.org/ - The National Child Traumatic Stress Network; provides information about trauma, evidence-based treatment approaches, and offers resources.

https://cptsdfoundation.org/cptsd-resources/ - CPTSD Foundation and access to real-time support. CPTSD is complex post-traumatic stress disorder that happens after repeated abuses/traumatic events, often childhood trauma.

Headspace app

https://narcissistabusesupport.com/

Guided Meditations by Sharon Salzberg (online). The video on YouTube is called *Meditation: Sharon Salzberg* and was recorded in 2014.

https://www.nctsn.org - Great information on trauma. They

have the most content on trauma of any organization. They are constantly putting out trainings to advance people's understanding of trauma and its impacts.

https://www.medicalnewstoday.com/articles/trauma#-causes - Helpful information about the nature and types of trauma.

https://www.verywellmind.com/identify-and-cope-with-emotional-abuse-4156673 - Emotional abuse can be difficult to understand and this site explains it fairly well.

For more resources in your journey to rise, go to www.resolvetorise.com.

ACKNOWLEDGMENTS

I would like to take a moment to thank the many people who were instrumental in making this long-held belief that I would write a book a reality. I'm going to do the best I can to ensure I mention everyone who played a role.

First, to my family members who listened to me read excerpts, asked questions, suggested edits, and celebrated every step along the journey, nudging me onward. I thought they would have begged out at some point, but my requests were always met with eager willingness to help.

To Brand Builders Group and specifically:

To Macy Robison, the best brand strategist I could have gotten! You pointed me in the right direction, gently redirected me at times, talked me off the ledge when I reviewed my first content evaluation, and gave me encouragement every time we met.

To Hilary Billings for helping me frame out my book. Your story is such an inspiration!

To Rory and AJ Vaden for living out your own purpose and constructing frameworks that enabled me to write my book!

To Martha Temple and Erin Hatzikostas for making time to meet and getting me connected to content and individuals who could help me along the way!

To Susan Cottrell, Kathy Carberry, and Dordy Pierre-Paul for listening to and reading content and spurring me on. Susan, you helped me see I needed to apologize less and reinforced my belief in my dream. Kathy, you encouraged me so many times and celebrated my progress with me. Dordy, you've been a great sojourner as you wrote and published your own work at the same time; your transparency was a real blessing.

To Barbara Thomas, who said, "Lilli, you should write a book! What you just read to me moved me." That got the wheels rolling in taking my dreams and making them reality!

To Scribe Media:

To Rikki for enthusiastically kicking off this incredible journey from manuscript to published book!

To Mikey for quarterbacking the entire progress and holding my hand through every step of the journey!

To John for providing thoughtful and impactful content edits honestly and with compassion.

To Derek for finding exactly the right cover art to express the beautiful result of healing the broken parts.

To Erin for taking 33,000 words and condensing it into eight sentences that describe the heart and soul of *Resolve to Rise*. And making me sound great! Your skills are remarkable!

And others who did copyedits, grammar and punctuation, and interior layout, making sure everything was in tiptop shape for publishing!

To the Magnificent 7 (My executive development program cohort...the best one ever), and specifically to Sasha and Ed who hosted me while I narrated my book in California.

And to many more who have believed in me and encouraged me along the way. I am so grateful to have so many friends, family and colleagues supporting me!

ABOUT THE AUTHOR

LILLI CORRELL is a Fortune-6 healthcare executive and licensed counselor. A dedicated champion of patient-centered solutions within the healthcare industry, she has spoken to crowds of thousands about the patient experience and has been featured in Golden News Wire, Open Minds, Mental Health America, and The National Association of State Mental Health Programs Directors.

Through her signature combination of intellect, insight, experience, and compassion, Lilli Correll offers powerful lessons that can help anyone rise above their circumstances and create their own unlimited success. Learn more at resolvetorise.com.